#We*Are*Rent

Rent

Humans evolved by working to create a
unique flow of energy – Rent – which
they pooled in their bodies and minds
to foster their aesthetic and spiritual
sensibilities. Rent is the living tissue of
our humanity, from which emerged the
Social Galaxy. When Rent is privatised,
the Social Galaxy begins to collapse.
To save humanity we must reclaim Rent.

#We*Are*Rent

Book 1

Capitalism, Cannibalism and
why we must outlaw Free Riding

FRED HARRISON

Land
Research
Trust

First published in 2021 by
Land Research Trust
7 Kings Road
Teddington
TW11 OQB, UK

Land
Research
Trust

landresearchtrust.org

British Library Cataloguing in Publication Data
A CIP catalogue record of this book is available
from the British Library

ISBN 978-0-9956351-9-7

Design by Ian Kirkwood
www.ik-design.co.uk

Printed by IngramSpark

Dedication

Dr Mason Gaffney
(1923-2020)
Professor of Economics, University of California

Sir Kenneth Jupp, MC
(1917–2004)
Judge in the English High Court

Dr George Miller
(1941-2007)
Professor of Epidemiology

#We*Are*Rent

Book 1

Capitalism, Cannibalism and why we must outlaw Free Riding

Contents

INTRODUCTION

Three Theses and the Great Reset

WE no longer have a choice. Humanity has arrived at a crossroads. At stake is our species. To survive we must move beyond the dual between capitalism and socialism. To relaunch onto the evolutionary path into the future we must learn from the hard-won lessons of the past.

Feudalism was spawned by the collapse of the classical civilisations. Socialism was spawned by the breakdown of capitalism. Neither feudalism nor socialism would have been incubated but for the exhaustion of the pre-existing social formations. Populations were parked into these stop-gap arrangements while awaiting the recovery of cultural evolution.

In 2020, as nations were decimated by a killer virus from China, people appealed for "no return to business-as-usual". That desire was expressed by David Malpass, the President of the World Bank Group: "Countries will need to prepare for a different economy post-Covid".[1] The *Financial Times* recorded that discontent "threatened to spill over into demands for total systemic change".[2]

It is not possible to deliver change on the basis of the ideas that prevail among the academics and politicians who shape public

---

1. IMF Press Release 20/254 https://www.imf.org/en/News/
2. Editorial (2020), "Bidenomics can preserve support for capitalism", *Financial Times*, October 23.

v

opinions and policies. No practical vision exists with which to chart a course out of the dead-end arrangements into which all nations are locked. That is why we need to formulate the fundamental principles on which societies may be redesigned. Despite a very narrow window of opportunity within which to initiate action, there is hope.

The precondition for a radical redesign of society, however, is an understanding of what it means to be human. To navigate the empirical evidence that spans two million years, I provide, a comprehensive theory of human evolution. This equips us to apply the principles that would lay the foundations for a social paradigm fit for the 21st century.

Our starting point is an appraisal of what it took for one branch of the primate species to evolve into humanity. Based on that knowledge, I contend that people would be liberated to decide how best to reconfigure their communities. The politics of how this could be achieved is the subject of Book 2. If agreement on those foundation principles can be extended to encompass the global community of nations, a new epoch in the evolution of our species would be initiated (Book 3). For the first time in history, *Homo sapiens* – armed with its own evolutionary blueprint – would be united to forge a future within the terms of peace and prosperity for everyone. This will only happen if we stop trying to patch up the mortal flaws in western capitalism and eastern socialism. Only then can we meaningfully ask: what may society look like after Covid-19?

Deviation from the evolutionary blueprint caused the collapse of earlier civilisations. To avoid that fate befalling western civilisation, we need to understand the role played by the unique source of energy which animated the evolution of our species. That energy is what the classical economists called *economic rent*. I shall denote this stream of resources as Rent.

Three indictments

When the flue pandemic struck in 1918, killing tens of millions of people worldwide, the socialist model was still lurking in the shadows of people's minds, waiting to be tried and tested. It was tried. It failed the test. That option is no longer credible (Box 1).

Box 1 **Post-socialist China**

At the 99th anniversary congress, in July 2020, Chinese Communist Party President-for-Life Xi Jinping claimed that their success at combating the coronavirus pandemic "fully demonstrated the clear superiority of Communist Party leadership and our socialist system". That was the fiction that sought to rationalise a brutal authoritarian regime. It

- ► employed concentration camps to "re-educate" (i.e., brainwash) millions of Muslim Uighurs into conforming to the party line;

- ► repressed Hong Kong citizens who dared to contemplate the possibility of an alternative politics to fulfil their aspirations; and

- ► intensified military threats against Taiwan in a bid to complete Mao's war against the first republic (formed in 1911), which sought a future based on the evolutionary model which is the subject of this book.

To sustain itself, an alien culture must coerce the collective consciousness of the people. The Communist Party's method is illustrated in Hong Kong's education system. Textbooks are being revised – censured – to remove awkward facts embodied in the liberal studies curriculum.* This is a mind-bending project that may be studied in real time. There is no future for humanity in the social model enforced by Beijing with the aid of military might.

* Nicolle Liu and Joe Leahy (2020), "Beijing targets Hong Kong schools in ideological clampdown", *Financial Times*, October 10.

This time is different. The Covid-19 pandemic convinced people of the need to reconstitute their working arrangements. Something novel had to be innovated.

But we cannot afford to devote time to dead-end experiments. Defensive strategies against the existential crises are required. Those strategies must be consistent with the structural reforms that need to be implemented if we are to forestall the social, environmental and demographic threats that are converging on a single point in time.

That a qualitative departure from present arrangements is necessary is attested to by the fact that governments are incapable of learning the lessons from social catastrophes of even the recent past, like the 2008 financial crisis. Governments and their distinguished and well-meaning professors continue to frame the post-pandemic prospects in terms derived from within capitalism. If their analytical models prevail, the outcome will be a catastrophic breakdown that no-one intends, but which is prescribed by the logic of the culture that dominates our lives. That assertion will be met with incredulity! That is why nations need to embark on a listen-and-learn conversation in which everyone may participate. Democratic consent is needed to support realistic policy options. The context for a radical reappraisal of current arrangements is needed . My contribution takes the form of three indictments.

Indictment I

Politicians who administer democratic governments wilfully cause the deaths of citizens every year. The deaths are on a pandemic scale, the consequence of an intrinsic feature of government revenue systems. The outcomes are intentional.

Taxes as championed by politicians burden people's lives to the point where many of them become the "excess deaths" for which no-one is held accountable. This tragedy is avoidable.

The benign fiscal alternative has been tried, tested, and authoritatively endorsed as the correct way to fund public services. There is no practical or moral reason for not reforming revenue systems so that everyone may be free to live full lives. And yet, politicians wilfully continue to use deadly financial tools for which they are not held responsible.

Indictment II

Fiscal policies are the root cause of global economic crises in all of their forms, social, demographic and environmental. Taxation, through the distortions they cause to people's lives and social systems, has pushed humanity up to the precipice of a deep vortex. There can be no retreat without transforming the way governments fund public services.

Government responsibility for the existential crises is camouflaged by shifting the blame on to individuals. This diverts attention away from the role of the state, the behaviour of policymakers, and taxation.

Indictment III

Tax policies were devised to accommodate free riding. This term is employed by anthropologists to identify antisocial behaviour. Humanity is now in thrall to the culture of free riding.

The economic term for free riding is "rent seeking". The people in power intentionally propagate this behaviour by their adherence to conventional tax policies. The onus, therefore, is on the public to insist on an audit that holds accountable those who abuse the power that has been entrusted to them.

The net income

The organic remedy is a single fiscal reform. By recovering the Rent of the commons to fund public services, a new synergy would emerge to empower people to organically amend the behaviour that damages both the fabric of humanity and the natural environment.

Rent is the value that remains after deducting the wages of labour and the profits from capital formation and enterprise. In its social form, Rent enables society to flourish. In its privatised form, Rent becomes a malevolent anti-evolutionary force.

This is a mono-causal explanation for our socially-significant problems. The people in power will seek to deride it as a simplistic distortion of reality. Academic economists ought to be able to adjudicate on this issue. That most of them are unable to do so, however, stems from the defects in the mathematical tools which they employ. Their theoretical models are detached from reality – not least, because one of the three components of economic activity (land) has been made to disappear.[3]

I am obliged to provide the evidence in support of this single-cause model. I have to demonstrate that socially significant problems originated in the culture that was spawned to serve the privatisation of Rent. Think of a rock thrown into a still pond. The ripples radiate outwards. Each wave diminishes in force. If we focus on the outer ripple, we think it was "caused" by the waves that came before it. We need to focus our gaze on the rock as it plunges into the water, and then trace the ripples. The transmission mechanisms must be shown to work through the generations that spanned five centuries.

---

3. A technical account of the detached-from-reality nature of post-classical economic models is offered by Cambridge economist Tony Lawson in *Reorienting Economics* (2003), London: Routledge, and "Mathematical Modelling and Ideology in the Economics Academy", *Economic Thought* (1), 2012.

The original rock-in-the-pool intervention was the systematic appropriation of the commons. This dispossessed people of their traditional access rights to the means that sustained their lives.

Figure 1 **Four tributaries from a single source**

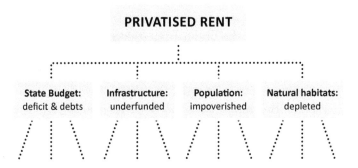

I must prove that, when net income is privatised, it pollutes – via a thousand and one streams – the psychic, social and ecological condition of the population from which it is extracted (Fig. 1). The impacts are most immediately visible in the realms of politics, on social infrastructure, and within personal lives, from where they are transmitted throughout the social and natural environments. I will show that, as this process unfolds, there is an incremental depletion of the pillars that support the social structure.

The cumulative impact of such trends leads inexorably to the collapse of civilisation. Students of past civilisations suggest that such "predicaments" become unpredictable and irreversible, for which "there are no solutions".[4] If that was the reality in

---

4. Pablo Servigne and Raphael Stevens (2020), *How Everything Can Collapse*, London: Polity Press, p.128.

previous epochs, it is not the case today. We *can* redesign our communities, even in the midst of the turmoil that will escalate in the next few years.

The historical evidence that supports my mono-causal explanation is so extensive, and seemingly complex, that we can be easily misled. To assist in marshalling the evidence, I offer three theses.

Three theses

To penetrate society, the original free riders had to deploy both overt violence and covert manipulation. By these means, they created a culture of cheating which concealed the root cause of the pathologies that were imposed on people. It was only a matter of time before the tipping point would be reached, beyond which it would no longer be possible to reverse the decline into existential obliteration. Our world is now pivoting on that tipping point.

Thesis I

In Europe, the privatisation of land that was traditionally held in common began in earnest in the 16th century. People were cheated of their rights. The cheats were rewarded with the privatisation of the Rent that people created through their cooperative activities. To sustain this behaviour, society was co-opted and turned against people's best interests.

Feudal aristocrats did not seek to control land as an end in itself. They had no intention of working in the fields! The land grabs were the essential first step to claiming the Rent of rural and urban locations. That Rent is the value of the services delivered by nature and society.

Thesis II

To protect and enhance their privileges, the self-certified landowners had to capture the power of the state, to gain control over its finances. By minimising the tax-take, the Rent

of land was maximised. That tax regime disabled society's immune systems. The collateral damage includes the erosion of communal resilience and economic productivity.

The UK will serve as the primary case study in Book 1, because it exercised more influence over the shape and content of the modern world than any other country. Free riding was embedded across the world through colonialism.

Thesis III

The victory of the rent-seekers of old is pyrrhic. Their culture has morphed into its cannibalistic phase and has corroded the living tissue of humanity to the point where modern human beings are no longer sustainable.

For the first time in history, humans are united by a common culture. The European West can be distinguished from the Asian East, the rich Global North from the poor Global South. But uniting everyone on Earth is that form of behaviour that originated in Europe five centuries ago. Colonialism came to a formal end in the 20th century, but free riding was retained in newly independent nations. Given the integrated nature of our world, the existential crisis now threatens our species. Book 1 tracks the steps taken to reach this catastrophic end.

By probing the historical facts to test my three theses, the contours of an authentic social paradigm emerges.

The authenticity standard

We live in a "post-truth" world. People do not know who to trust. To negotiate this treacherous situation, we need clarity in our language, for words are used to conceal awkward truths. If we want sound public policy we must eliminate linguistic drivel. This is illustrated by the word "wealth". This is employed in debates as if its definition was not controversial (wealth is what "rich" people own). The concept has become an obstacle to clarifying the terms of good governance and the responsibilities of the individual.

The problem with the word wealth was highlighted by economist Joseph Stiglitz, one of the very few distinguished academics willing to risk unpopularity by speaking the truth. He declares:

> "One cannot understand what is happening to inequality of wealth without taking into account the growth of rents".[5]

To appreciate why this is a startling observation, we need to retrace our steps to the beginning of economics as a social science.

In the 18th century, the classical economists explained that production was based on three factors: land, labour and capital. By the 20th century, land disappeared as a distinct category. It was buried under the heading of "capital". The distinctive characteristics of land (and so their implications) were eviscerated from the gaze of generations of students. Why and how land was made to disappear from the analytical models employed by economists will become clear as our narrative unfolds.

Thus, as the prelude to reforming our social behaviour, we need a linguistic clean-up operation. When carefully scrutinised, for example, the concepts of capitalism and socialism are exposed as inauthentic social systems. They are anchored in ideologies that had to consecrate their structures of power in the blood of millions of people.

My concept of authenticity is derived from the evolutionary process in which early humans cooperated to invest in their biology, psychology and spirituality – what became the legacy assets of humanity. Prehistorical peoples enforced, through their customs and practices, behaviour that sustained their evolution.

5. Joseph E. Stiglitz (2015), "The Origins of Inequality, and Policies to Contain It", *National Tax Journal*, 68(2), p. 437.

The implicit social contract took the form of a commitment to give new-born babies the opportunity to one day work for their living without having to accommodate the demands of free riders.

An authentic social system is one that honours as sacred a new-born baby's birth rights, coupled with the responsibility of adults to protect those rights for future generations.

A child born to a slave (say, on a plantation in the American South) was never going to participate in a humane social system. Likewise, a child born to a tenant farmer in 18th century France was not going to mature within a community that conformed to the values defined by the evolutionary history of humanity. Those societies placed the demands of free riders above the needs of anyone else. When the evolutionary contract was ruptured (as occurred during colonial times), the vitality was driven out of communities. The scarring effects were inscribed on bodies, on psyches and on customs and practices. We can observe the outcomes among the opioid dependent Inuit communities in Canada and among Aboriginal tribes in Australia. We can also witness that scarring in the deprivation that is visible in towns in northern England and across the rust-belt of the United States, and in the slums around the cities of South Africa.

I will amplify my model of an authentic social paradigm as my contribution to the reconstruction of communities according to the norms of efficiency and justice. If the Rent model withstands scrutiny, we would have at our disposal a viable alternative narrative to the capitalist and socialist ideologies. That would release us from the political constipation that has reduced governance to a state of policy paralysis.

The transition away from free riding can be managed on terms that would rescue the West. The pre-condition for the elevation to a new kind of civilisation is the willingness of people to authorise reforms to the pricing mechanisms in both the public and private sectors. That consent, at present, does not exist.

The Power of Three

Because my narrative departs from the conventional wisdoms, readers need to exercise caution. In assessing my claim that western civilisation is facing extinction, the reader is entitled to know the basis on which I offer my judgements. I supplement the common sense that we all share with the technique that I acquired as a journalist. I call it the Power of Three.

By profession, I specialised in the investigation of anti-social and criminal behaviour. This is a hazardous business. Get the facts wrong and one's newspaper risked punitive libel damages. My editor's lawyers obliged me to favour provable facts over purple prose. The lawyers insisted that one piece of evidence to support an accusation was not sufficient. In a libel court, that evidence could be explained away as an accident. Nor were two pieces of evidence sufficient: they could be explained away as a coincidence. Three pieces of documented evidence, however, revealed a pattern of behaviour that could be presented for scrutiny in the court of public opinion.

The challenge before all of us is enormous. Our world needs a Great Reset. I will explain how we can prevent the termination of the most fantastic experiment in the 14 billion year history of the universe. Thanks to that extra pool of energy that our earliest ancestors invested in themselves, as Rent, we can work out how to restore order in place of chaos. So I offer this volume as a celebration, not as an epitaph, of our humanity. Book 1 describes the process that has brought us to the crises of the 21st century. Book 2 explains how the nations of Europe may begin to reverse this crisis by reconstituting politics and the laws of the land. Book 3 offers an aspirational prospectus for humanity, based on a revised arrangement for global trade and by relaunching the co-evolutionary relationships with other species in our shared habitats.

We should not complacently assume that our species will continue to enjoy its privileged status on Earth. Like all the other autochthonous creatures – born from the earth – humans did not originate with the aid of some supernatural act. But humans did manage to create a unique space of their own. That space emerged in the universe because our earliest ancestors learned how to embody the gravitational attraction of Rent into a self-perpetuating system.

Hitherto, scholars lacked a metric with which to track the rise and fall of civilisations. Rent is that metric. It offers, *inter alia*, a forensic insight into the direction and scale of change of the Social Galaxy, the resilience of a population's moral fabric and the capacity of governance – all summed in a single number.

Rent makes the Good Life possible for everyone if we put our minds and morals to work. Knowing that, however, is of little use without human agency (the ability to act). By freeing ourselves from the noose that the free riders of old wove around our minds, we can act on the basis of an authentic freedom. But to move in that direction, we first have to confront the primary existential question: who owns Rent?

We do.

Because #WeAreRent.

Fred Harrison

London
December, 2020

Metaphysics and Monkey Business

According to the laws of nature, we humans should not exist. It is as if, as aliens, we stumbled on this universe and colonised one of its planets.

We exist because of one earth-shattering discovery. While other species remained locked into nature, our earliest ancestors learnt how to forestall one of the laws that regulate the universe. They unravelled the secret of the 2nd Law of Thermodynamics. That empowered them to create a unique flow of energy – *Rent*. Rent, as we shall see, is the sum of resources that exceed what was needed for biological subsistence. Those resources gave early humans the power to create what became humanity.

Our earliest ancestors could not articulate the metaphysics of Rent. That task was left for us.

Metaphysics is the branch of philosophy that is concerned with understanding the nature of, and the relations among, the things that exist. By understanding Rent, we are equipped with the insights for decoding the origins and nature of the greatest invention in the universe – the Social Galaxy (Box P.1).

Employing their intuition and the method of trial and error, early humans worked out practical answers to advance each phase of their evolutionary journey out of nature. By this means, they began to pose metaphysical questions for us.

▶ *How* did humans challenge the laws of nature?

▶ *Why* was it necessary to live a spiritual life?

▶ *What* would constitute an authentic system of power?

▶ *When* should customs and practices be redesigned?

▶ *Who* should be trusted to guide communities?

If, in antiquity, the priests and princes who guided their civilisations were able to answer such questions, they might have avoided the collapse of their societies.

Because the evolutionary vitality of Rent has been eroded, the Social Galaxy is orbiting at an ever slower rate. It is pivoting on the precipice of a black hole. Emergency action is needed. Our task is to explain how we can sustain and enrich what has

---

Box P.1 **Formation of the Social Galaxy**

Armed with the special power that early humans created, it became possible to construct a unique living space, a self-sustaining Social Galaxy. There are more than two trillion galaxies in the universe, but only one Social Galaxy. That galaxy became possible because the earliest timespace travelling humans created techniques that forestalled the dystopian outcomes of the 2nd Law of Thermodynamics. They achieved this by investing their net resources in their

i) *biological evolution:* reshaping the body's head (to encase a larger brain), and an upright posture to roam across open spaces;

ii) *mental attributes:* evolving the psychological and spiritual sensibilities that expanded the world of the imagination; and

iii) *material infrastructure:* from rudimentary hand tools to the satellite command centres that now direct missions to Mars.

For the Social Galaxy to co-exist with the universe, an implicit contract was evolved to harmonise the laws of nature with the social laws that regulated the behaviour of humans.

---

mutated into a global civilisation. If we arm ourselves with a revitalised Rent, the existential threats that pervade life in the 21st century can be contained. Europe is the place to start because it is the epicentre of moral, mental and material fatigue.

The multi-dimensional character of Rent fulfils three needs. First, it is the analytical tool for facilitating diagnosis, prognosis and prescription. Second, it is the moral compass which defines personal rights and responsibilities, and delineates the borders between the public and private spheres of life. Third, it is the material means for correcting the socially significant problems that embroil all of us.

The route to understanding Rent entails a detour back in time. The story of the rise of humankind reveals the primal nature of Rent. The urgency with which we need to approach this exercise stems from the abuse of Rent, which has thrown humanity's unique evolutionary journey into reverse. The multiple existential crises that have now surfaced can only be addressed by the change to behaviour that would emerge organically from adherence to this principle:

"Keep what you create, and pay for what you receive."

Few people would disagree with that rule, but adopting it will entail a great deal of soul searching. Resetting the foundations of society implies a profound moral challenge. That is why the process must begin with cathartic conversations that are honestly informed by the relevant facts. Many obstacles will have to be overcome, because we are hostages of a culture of cheating that has had five centuries to manipulate our minds and shape our institutions. The outcome is societies traumatised by the original free riders. Every part of humanity and the Social Galaxy has been polluted, pushing us through the depletion zone to the tipping point (Figure P.1).

Figure P.1 **Organic Components of the Social Galaxy**

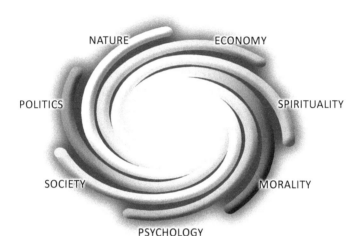

The Social Galaxy is a fragile creation. Its vitality depends on continuous renewal. Sufficient Rent must be produced to secure genetic evolution, aesthetic sensibilities, spiritual fulfilment and empirical – and now scientific – knowledge. When Rent was privatised, that fabric of humanity was undermined. One indicator of that corrosion is mental ill-health.

Privatised Rent is starving our minds of nourishment.

The scale and existential implications of mental ill-health today is grave, according to Dr Michael Crawford, a Visiting Professor at London's Imperial College, London (Chelsea and Westminster Hospital Campus).

[T]he escalation of mental ill-health…is a more serious threat to the sustainability of humanity than global warming. This in no way diminishes the importance of climate change but emphasizes the extreme gravity of what we are facing. If mental ill health continues to escalate then it is painfully obvious that humanity is finished. It is as simple as that. It is incredible that food and agricultural policies have progressed without any attention never mind prioritising the nutrient needs for the brain. The ignorance is astounding. It is the brain which makes us different from monkeys and apes. Nature treats human prenatal development as her priority. She devotes 70% of all the energy the mother puts into foetal development to brain growth. It is all so painfully obvious yet serving the brain is nowhere.[1]

To test my narrative, we need to locate it in its evolutionary context. Comparing humans with our nearest cousins, the chimpanzees, sheds light on what it takes to be a healthy person. First, we begin by addressing two issues. (1) We need to remove a misunderstanding about the quality of the lives of hunter-gatherers. Anthropologists characterise them as living at the level of subsistence. (2) We need to recover an understanding of the significance of the way in which hunter-gatherers distributed the product of their labour.

The nourishing of humanity

Humans and chimpanzees share their DNA with 1% difference. And yet, there is a world of difference between life in the forests of Africa and South America, and the civil life of pre-agricultural humans.

Chimpanzees live a day-to-day existence to keep their bodies alive to procreate another day. They do not work to produce anything over and above what they need to sustain themselves biologically.

People who lived by hunting and gathering produced more than their subsistence. The net flow of energy was invested in the codes of conduct that increased the complexity of social life,

1. Michael Crawford, email to Rev. Paul Nicolson, Feb. 9, 2020. For a full elaboration of this thesis, see Michael Crawford and David Marsh, *The Brain under Siege*, forthcoming.

and in the knowledge that would equip them to migrate out of Africa and into new habitats. Grahame Clark (1907-1995), the archaeologist of prehistory at Cambridge University, contrasted prehistoric people with other species by emphasising "the effort they put into matters over and beyond what is needed for their biological survival".[2]

Prehistoric people were not living just to survive biologically. They were embarked on a unique journey. They were combining the resource endowments of their habitats with the assets that they were accumulating within their bodies and communities, to evolve further away from nature. None of that could be achieved if they were living at the level of "bare subsistence". And yet, the impression conveyed by the literature on pre-agricultural societies is that our ancestors were "primitive" and were living on the margin of existence. But varying with each level of development, pre-agricultural societies were rich – and getting richer. The richness was not just in material artefacts, but growth in the assets that define humanity – their minds, their aesthetic and spiritual sensibilities, and their social institutions. Those assets were transmitted inter-generationally. To adjust our perceptions of those people to realistic levels, we need to start where it all began, with the primate family.

Chimpanzees shared with the earliest humans the mental capacity for communication. That trait originated about 40 million years ago,[3] and is one of the reasons why primatologists say that humans are not unique.[4] But chimpanzees, for example, did not expand their minds to the point where they could invest for the

---

2. Grahame Clark (1992), *Space, Time and Man*, Cambridge: Cambridge University Press, p.54.
3. Stuart K. Watson *et al* (2020), "Nonadjacent dependency processing in monkeys, apes, and humans", *Science Advances* (6), p.3. https://doi.org/10.1126/sciadv.abb0725
4. Niccolo Caldararo (2009), "The tendency to make man an exception", in Emil Potocki and Juliusz Krasinski (eds), *Primatology: Theories, Methods and Research*, New York: Nova Science Publishers.

future. They did not learn how to *purposefully accumulate* resources for investment in what we now call the *common good*. A prime illustration of the difference is in the tools used to gather food.

Chimpanzees pick up stones to crack the shells that give them access to nourishing nuts. They pick up twigs to poke down holes, to extract juicy termites. The rocks and twigs are then thrown away. But as was noted by Kenneth Oakley (1911–1981), an English anthropologist, palaeontologist and geologist, "This is a far cry from the systematic making of stone tools, the earliest known examples of which evidently required much premeditation, a high order of skill and an established tradition".

Humans fashioned their tools. Stones were chipped into sharp implements which served as daggers and scrapers. Branches cut from trees were trimmed into arrows and spears that could be projected long distances. Labour power and ingenuity were invested in what became the first forms of capital equipment. The primary lesson was being learnt: rocks and twigs could be transformed into instruments that increased the productivity of labour. But that capital had to be conserved and renewed, to prevent the 2nd Law from reclaiming them in a degraded condition. That entailed the expenditure of specialised work to preserve the initial investment. The care devoted to tool-making blended with the aesthetics of craftsmanship. Oakley reviewed the collection of tools assembled in the British Museum, and noted how tool-making interacted with "sympathetic magic", which was "a kind of primitive scientific theory". Combined with learning how to control fire, humans took "the greatest step forward in the direction of gaining freedom from the dominance of environment".[5]

Anthropologists and zoologists hypothesise a variety of explanations to account for this evolutionary journey: growth of human intelligence was provoked by the development of technology and

---

5. Kenneth P. Oakley (1975), *Man the Tool-maker*, London: British Museum, pp.2, 83-85.

tools; spatial memory was required to visualise the food content of a territory; and sociality – the increasingly complex relationships that enabled individuals to live in harmony with others. Even so, the collective wisdom of the scholars continues to treat those early humans as living "at the level of bare subsistence", as Oakley put it on page 89 of his elegantly illustrated study of tool-making.

Subsistence implies that there is nothing left over for use beyond sustaining rudimentary biological existence. This misrepresents the nature of humanity, and the significance of the extra effort devoted to producing more than what was required to meet biological needs.

English primatologist Jane Goodall characterised the tools employed by chimpanzees as "subsistence technology".[6] She analysed tool-using in these terms:

> If the object is used successfully, then the animal achieves a goal in which a number of instances would not have been possible without the aid of the tool. Some of the purposes include: (1) use of thorn or twig as a "skewer", (2) use of spine or twig as a probe, (3) use of the bark "plug", and (4) use of stones and rocks. Tool-using behaviour in primates falls into two distinct categories: the use of objects as weapons in aggressive contexts; and in non-agonistic contexts for obtaining food for investigation and body care.[7]

Entranced by the primates who go about their business with the aid of twigs and stones, primatologists overlook the one distinction which made the world of difference between chimps and early humans. The tools employed by humans enabled them to increase the productivity of their labour. And yet, those tools were characterised as "subsistence technology" by Nicholas Humphrey, the English neuro-psychologist, who studied the evolution of primate intelligence and consciousness in mountain gorillas in

6. Jane Goodall (1964), "Tool-using and aimed throwing in a community of free-living chimpanzees", *Nature* (201) p.1264.
7. Jane Van Lawick-Goodall (1971), Tool-Using in Primates and Other Vertebrates, *Advances in the Study of Behavior* (3). https://doi.org/10.1016/S0065-3454(08)60157-6

Rwanda. In an influential article published in 1976, he described the business of socialising as "unproductive". This "time given up to unproductive social activity" was at the expense of "basic subsistence activities".[8] But those social activities were productive; furthermore, they were only possible because people were capable of producing more than their subsistence needs.

The characterisation of evolutionary history in terms of biological subsistence evokes fatally misleading impression of human evolution. This, in turn, fosters the notion that resources can be extracted without the *quid pro quo* of having to work for them. That is the basis of the doctrine of the free lunch, which must be challenged. Our guide on scientific issues will be physicist Albert Einstein. If there are doubts about the objectivity of our judgements, Einstein can be trusted to assess the merits of the evidence.

Enter the Demon

To break away from the primate family, our ancestors had to work to add value to the pool of Rent. The first clause in the implicit contract with nature was that beneficiaries had to work for the resources that they extracted from their habitats. There was no free lunch.

Our ancestors understood that principle. It is cast aside today by those who indulge in free riding.

Free riding relies on the doctrine of "living without working". That notion is rationalised by the hypothesis of entitlement. So embedded is this attitude that we need to remind ourselves not just of its social history but also how science unwittingly came to endorse it, with the suggestion that we can harvest nature without labouring for the rewards. A major illustration is offered by the work of James Clerk Maxwell (1831–1879).

8. Nicholas K. Humphrey (1988), "The social function of intellect", in Richard Byrne and Andrew Whitten (eds.), *Machiavellian Intelligence*, Oxford: Oxford University Press, p.21.

Einstein certifies the significance of Maxwell's work, by acknowledging that his special theory of relativity "owes its origin to Maxwell's equations of the electromagnetic field".[9] In Einstein's view, "One scientific epoch ended and another began with James Clerk Maxwell".[10]

Maxwell, a bearded Scot who taught students in the universities of Cambridge, London and Aberdeen, devised the use of thought experiments. Relevant for our purpose is his account of an experiment in *Theory of Heat* (1871). It featured the problem of entropy – the way in which energy, or matter, degrades from order to disorder under the influence of the 2nd Law.

Maxwell imagined the possibility of intervening in the way hot and cold molecules in the universe were distributed. His aim was to block the flow of energy from an ordered to the disorderly state, to sustain the orderly state. To achieve what he said was impossible, Maxwell invented "a finite being". William Thomson (1824-1907), a professor of natural philosophy at Glasgow University, named that entity Maxwell's Demon.[11] The name stuck. Maxwell vested the Demon with intelligence and free will, enabling it to observe and direct individual molecules of matter.

The Demon's first outing was in a letter Maxwell wrote to a friend. He described how an experiment could be conducted by using a box separated into two compartments.

> Now conceive of a finite being who knows the paths and velocities of all the molecules by simple inspection, but *who can do no work except open and close a hole in the diaphragm by means of a slide without mass*.[12]

---

9. Albert Einstein (1949); *Autobiographical Notes*, 1966, La Salle, IL: Open Court, p.59.
10. Basil Mahon (2004), *The Man who Changed Everything*, London: John Wiley.
11. Sir William Thomson (1874), "Kinetic Theory of the Dissipation of Energy", *Nature*, April 9, p.444. https://zapatopi.net/kelvin/papers/kinetic_theory.html
12. Brian Clegg (2019), *Professor Maxwell's Duplicitous Demon*, London: Icon, pp.126-127. Emphasis added.

By this means, the hot and cold molecules would be separated. This would slow up the process of entropy, thereby deferring the impact of the 2nd Law.

Twice, in his *Theory of Heat*, Maxwell insisted that the experiment was being conducted "without the expenditure of work".[13] And yet, as he had to acknowledge, it would take the expenditure of labour power to open and close the hatch in the box, monitor the movement of individual molecules, and exercise judgement about when to intervene in the flow of molecules between the two compartments. Without those energy-consuming interventions, the 2nd Law would continue to operate unhampered, resulting in entropy.

For humanity to evolve, entropy had to be postponed. This could only be achieved through the expenditure of labour power. That labour power would make it possible to create the special flow of energy which became unique to the human species.

Maxwell could not conceive of how this might be accomplished without cheating. But the early humans who ventured out of the forests of Africa did resolve the problem. They became the Demons, with one exception: unlike Maxwell's finite being, they were mortal. They had to apply labour power to accomplish the impossible.

The earliest ancestors of *Homo sapiens* were climbing trees for a living some two million years ago.[14] One day, they abandoned the trees and migrated into the savannah grasslands on a journey through time and space. The genius of early humans was in devising a way to gravitate out of the monkey business. Somehow, they had conducted a real-world experiment that would transform planet Earth. But they had to devote labour power to achieve the

---

13. J.C. Maxwell (1872), *Theory of Heat*, 3rd edn., London: Longmans, Green, p.308.
14. Leoni Georgiou *et al* (2020), "Evidence for habitual climbing in a Pleistocene hominin in South Africa", Proceedings of the National Academy of Sciences, Feb. 18. www.pnas.org/cgi/doi/10.1073/pnas.1914481117

benefits, to create and store the energy that made it all possible. To achieve that level of productivity, they learnt to manipulate nature's 2nd Law. That could only be achieved by expanding the brain, which meant producing more sustenance than was needed by the chimps.

The intelligent mind

When the hominins began to expand the size of the energy-hungry brain, they were able to intensify their relationships with others, develop sophisticated techniques for making tools, and extend their knowledge of natural landscapes.

Today, when the body is at rest, the brain needs 20% to 25% of the body's overall energy consumption. That is 350 or 450 calories per day for the average woman or man. This makes the brain (which is only 2% of the body's overall weight) the most energy-expensive organ in the body.

To feed the expanding size of the brain, our ancestors had to expand the flow of the resources they consumed. In doing so, they were able to embark on the risky business of exploring new horizons. *They remained hunter-gatherers, but this was no longer a subsistence way of life.*

We may take, as the base line for subsistence, the needs of chimpanzees. They had to feed brains that weighed 40 grams. Over a period of 2m years, hominins grew into humans all the way through to *Homo sapiens* by expanding their brains to a weight of more than 1,400 grams (Figure P.2). To achieve this growth, there had to be a corresponding increase in productivity to produce more than what was required for biological survival.

That additional revenue was not hoarded by the individuals who produced it. It was shared by the evolutionary group that defined itself both genetically and socially. This continued right up to the 20th century. Anthropologists working in the field noted

Figure P.2 **Evolution of the human brain**

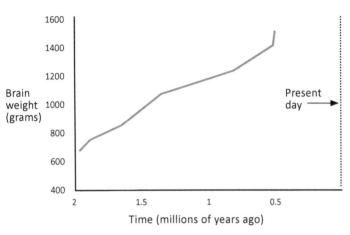

Source: Adapted from Robert Foley (1995), *Humans before Humanity*, Oxford: Blackwell, p.161.

how tribal people who still hunted and gathered employed codes of behaviour which were designed to equalise the resources within their communities. This was not primitive communism. While net resources were shared, "demand-sharing societies were simultaneously highly individualistic, where no one was subject to the coercive authority of anyone else, but at the same time were intensely egalitarian".[15]

The work ethic was combined with the sharing ethic. Without that combination, it would not have been possible to construct the Social Galaxy. This view of humanity yields vital insights that now ought to inform the social sciences. One issue relates to the metrics employed to track the growth of resources. In economics, gross domestic product (GDP) has been criticised as seriously

15. James Suzman (2010), *Work: A history of How We Spend Our Time*, London: Bloomsbury Circus, pp. 156.

deficient as a measure of performance. But the alternatives now being suggested are not framed in the practical terms that can be enshrined in law. One proposal is to track happiness as an indicator of well-being. Happiness was enshrined as an inalienable right in the US Declaration of Independence in 1776. For millions of people in America today, well-being falls well short of anything representing happiness. Is the explanation to be found in the way that Rent is privately appropriated, so that it is not shared?

Revisions are not only required for the social sciences, however. The Darwinian theory of evolution also needs to be re-visited (Box P.2).

Box P.2 **Man's best friend**

Humans engaged in an interactive evolutionary process that is more complex than the genetics-based model developed by Charles Darwin. His theory focused on biological adaptation to a neutral natural environment. It accounted for the evolution of other species, but it could not encompass human evolution. Humans adapted themselves not just to the resource endowments of their habitats, but were also challenged by their own creation of a social milieu, to which their offspring had to adapt. This was a dynamic process over which humans exercised some degree of choice.

The human environment included the co-evolution with other species. Five breeds of dogs, for example, were bred from the grey wolf around 130,000 years ago. Dogs served a triple purpose. Economically, they helped during the hunt for food. Psychologically, they provided pleasure for their owners. Biologically, they served as a source of food during times of scarcity.

As it is applied to humans, the theory of evolution needs to be modified if we are to correctly understand the making of *Homo sapiens*. The emergent knowledge would enable us to derive deeper insights for guiding the evolution of our species in the future.

The Social Galaxy

Without Rent, our ancestors would still be sharing the forests with chimpanzees.

By working to increase the size of the brain, it became possible to act purposefully, intentionally. As they matured their minds, the imagination generated explanations for their presence on the planet. The spiritual life provided the earliest system of rewards and punishments to reinforce the moral codes that regulated complex relationships in extended communities. All of this was made possible by the production and pooling of the net flow of resources, the Rent that elevated them out of the state of subsistence.

None of this could have happened without the self-discipline that enforced the work ethic. We shall show (Chapter 1) how pre-agricultural people suppressed the attitude of entitlement – the right to live without working, by exploiting the labour of others. Intuition served the hunter-gatherers well. They would have been bewildered by the feudal nobility's principle of privatising the Rent created by other people. We need to recover their wisdom if we wish to save our civilisation. In doing so, much of what currently perplexes us becomes intelligible. We need to understand that the aristocracy could only sustain their privileges by

- ▶ *controlling governance:* by designing the judicial system and state institutions to protect the culture of free riding;

- ▶ *controlling the economy:* by calibrating investment and entrepreneurialism to maximise the output of Rent; and

- ▶ *controlling minds:* by inhibiting the capacity to reason, to deter people from resisting the injustices being inflicted on them.

By these means, the capacity to effectively challenge the free rider hypothesis was neutralised. Societies were weakened to the point where they cannot now deal with stresses in the realms of

- ▶ *politics:* law-makers generate serious errors of administration, fostering popular distrust of those in power;

- ▶ **economics**: degraded systems of production create inequalities that animate prejudices such as racism; and

- ▶ *philosophy:* intellectuals fly false flag solutions instead of challenging inequities embedded in the laws of the land.

We all face the practical challenge of how to engage in the rehabilitation of the Social Galaxy. There are no short-cuts, no conjuring tricks by politicians or bloody upheavals favoured by revolutionaries. The rules need to be changed because, as Joseph Stiglitz put it, those rules "have all worked together to create a poorer-performing economy marked by greater rent seeking and greater inequality".[16] If change is to occur, the reforms must be based on democratic consent.

The moral challenge is immense. Few of us will admit that, like free riders, we are beneficiaries of the culture of cheating. As home owners, we have been co-opted by the culture of free riding into depriving others of the fruits of their labour. To admit this would be humiliating. That is why the capital gains derived from investing in the housing market are treated as having been earned by "hard work". Any challenge to this contention is met with indignation. The favourite rebuttal deployed by the guardians of the *status quo* is the mantra which subtly implies that the value embedded in residential property is earned by "hard working middle-class homeowners" (Box P.3).

16. Joseph Stiglitz (2020), "Conquering the Great Divide", *Finance & Development*, September, p.18.

Box P.3 **Cooking up a fortune?**

Home owners work for their wages, out of which they repay the mort-gages that they need to purchase their dwellings. Does that mean they earned the capital gains that arise when they sell their homes?

The economics of the residential market may be illustrated by a trans-action that featured in the British media in 2020. Famous TV chef Pru Leith offered her home for sale for a reported £10m. According to the news reports, the property was purchased in 1972 for £80,000.*

Were the capital gains earned by hard work? The original sum paid for the property needs to be adjusted for inflation and deducted from the resale price. In addition, the value of improvements to the property were funded out of earned income, and need to be taken into account. The difference – the capital gain - represents a value that did not materi-alise out of thin air. It was created by someone.

The net gains from the resale of dwellings cannot be attributed to the buildings (which depreciate). They represent the value of the locations. Those gains are not earned, but are transferred from others who did work to create them.

* https://www.dailymail.co.uk/news/article-8875791/Bake-star-Prue-Leith-puts-Cotswolds-manor-house-market-10million.html

The scientific breakthroughs of the 19th century in biology and sociology (as we shall see in Book 3) could have been combined with evolutionary economics to deliver a robust social paradigm. That would have transformed the prospects of people living through the Industrial Revolution. They would have been equipped to steer our world into an authentic state of freedom in the 20th century. The formulation of that narrative was the duty of philosophers. They had the skills to weave the evidence into a story that was accessible to people who were demanding the right to shape their future. The need was for an honest synthesis of the scientific disciplines.

That did not happen. Immanent enlightenment was exchanged for darkness.

The human faces of that darkness were displayed in the USA on November 3, 2020, when over 73 million Americans voted to keep Donald J. Trump in the White House. That was a self-destructive act which registered the tragic state to which western civilisation had been depleted. Most of Trump's adoring supporters (his "base") were victims of the culture that their hero symbolised. He was the archetype of the form of cheating that was responsible for their desperate economic plight, and which had aroused their distrust of mainstream politicians. But during the four years of Trump's presidency, his supporters were not provided with the tools to decode the arch rent seeker's behaviour, even though his motivation was in plain sight. This exposes two realities of existential significance.

1. The depth of penetration of the culture which has corrupted practically every nation in the world.

2. The scale of the crisis that must be challenged, if humanity is to be rescued.

If we are to free ourselves to interrogate the available policy choices, the historical context that brought about this state of affairs needs to be understood.

Our task, now, is to shed light on how humanity can gravitate back onto the path of evolution.

CHAPTER ONE

The Making of Humanity

We are Rent. Literally. Without Rent our primordial ancestors could not have traversed out of their primate origins and into the Neolithic age to become *Homo sapiens*. The transition was made possible because, intuitively, they acquired the wisdom to create and channel Rent into the fabric of their bodies and souls. That allocation of resources launched them on to a unique evolutionary pathway. But to complete that mission they had to formulate a primary law.

No cheating!

By honouring that law, they were able to accumulate and enhance enormous quantities of genetic and psychological material. By this means they carved out a unique space in the universe for a self-conscious species. But this success was contingent on one condition: everyone had to pull his and her weight.

There was no room for free riders.

It worked. Through biological adaptation and cultural innovation, spiritual sensibilities were evolved that inspired the moral codes of conduct which disciplined people's behaviour. The spirit of cooperation was nurtured, creating a fighting chance for the emergence of a new species on Earth.

This could not happen within the laws that regulated life on the planet. That is why proto-humans developed the capacity to construct something unique in the universe: a space within which they could over-ride one of the key laws of nature. The Social Galaxy was born.

It took a million years of genetic investment - the biological hardware - to facilitate the transition. Evolution of the cultural software was concentrated in a relatively short period of about 100,000 years. That achievement was based on Rent, the extra flow of energy that was the life-blood of the new super-organism in the universe. Without Rent, humans would not now be reaching for the stars.

For that outcome, we owe a debt-for-life to the creative genius of hundreds of generations of people who assumed the responsibility for creating and pooling that additional flow of energy that could be shared by everyone, to serve the common good. Guiding that process were the rules that allocated Rent to its appropriate uses. Those rules made possible the formation of complex cultures in new niches around the planet. Many routes to accomplishing this outcome overlapped.

- ► *In production*: channelling part of the material output into the common domain for everyone's benefit.

- ► *In reproduction*: formation of the extended family to transmit the legacy assets through the generations.

- ► *In socialisation*: devoting time and energy to the caring of neighbours and nurturing those in need.

This was how "man makes himself", in the term coined by the late V. Gordon Childe, a professor of archaeology at the University of Edinburgh. Honouring the rights and the corresponding responsibilities of being human was the process that renewed and enriched the flow of Rent in the emerging Social Galaxy.

That energy had to be continuously produced and invested in the evolution of assets in their multi-layered forms.

► *Psychology*: the mental outlook that extended the range of personal relationships through spiritual exploration and intellectual engagement.

► *Sociability*: the ritual practices that solidified communal relationships, such as remembering ancestors and celebrating the change of seasons.

► *Aesthetics*: the symbolic life that emerged in ceremonial clothing, bodily adornments, art and the linguistic representations of their aspirations.

Authority structures enforced the rules in challenging times (such as episodes of climate change) and equipped communities to adapt to strange places (in the quest for new niches). From parental authority through to clan chiefs and then the complex administrative mechanisms required by urban civilisation, the structures of power were imperative in securing wise decision-making and inclusive participation.

This was not a lonely journey through time and space. Early humans used their rules of conduct to co-evolve with other forms of life. Those codes secured balanced growth in relationships both within human communities, and in partnership with the other species whose habitats they shared.

Crucial to this process was the capacity to imagine new ways of living. It took time to establish and sustain the realm of the imagination, drawing first on the laws of nature, and then on the laws of society. Evolution originated with Darwinian principles of adaptation. That process of nature was supplemented with the flow of Rent, the creation of which was made possible by expanding brain size, jaw shape and upward gait. These changes liberated our earliest ancestors to stray beyond their original habitats, roaming both in their imaginations and what became the spatial migration out of Africa.

To increase the complexity of their lives and communities, they had to accumulate new knowledge to accelerate the production of Rent. This flow of energy made possible the emergence of the two personalities that were successfully fused to become the human constitution.

► *The template personality* was composed of the legacy assets that were inherited by individuals as their birthright.

Those assets were the products of the work and wisdom of working together for the common good. The assets came into existence as a result of the development of mental and aesthetic capacities. Those assets required the investment of resources that exceeded what individuals needed for biological subsistence. The willingness to produce and invest those resources in moral and spiritual sensibilities made possible the formation of humanity.

► *The personal characteristics* that people worked to create for themselves, and which distinguished them as unique beings.

These individual attributes of a person's specific circumstances (home life, education, friendships and resource endowments) shaped the persona that facilitated evolutionary progress.

This momentous process of a species coming into existence can be restated in classical economic concepts.

► The individual laboured to produce – and exclusively consume – the resources which sustained the procreative unit, the family: *Wages*.

► To aid their labour, people fashioned Capital equipment, the tools that had to be renewed by reinvesting part of production: *Profits*.

▶ After allowing for Wages and Profits, the net income measured the value of the services provided by nature and society: *Rent*.

Rent is not the commercial rent that we pay to hire an apartment or an automobile. That everyday concept of "rent" includes the capital costs of producing the dwelling or vehicle, which are rewarded with interest (popularly called profits). The concept of Rent employed here was defined by classical economists and is elaborated in Boxes 1.1 to 1.3.

Box 1.1 **The Rent of Nature**

Nature, in its pristine state, generates Rent that can be measured as a value that is distinct from wages. Two UK court cases illustrate the value attributed to the services of nature.

David Matthews, a scrap metal tycoon, chopped down 11 trees so that his property would benefit from extra light and space, the value of which was estimated at £135,500. That value was added to Matthews' home as a result of chain-sawing the trees. Despite the legal protection given to the 100-year-old trees, which included a mature oak, a beech and sweet chestnut, Matthews decided that his interests eclipsed those of nature and the community which granted the trees legal protection. He was punished with a fine and court costs of £32,000, and ordered to yield the £135,500 under a Proceeds of Crime Order.*

In the second case, Trevor Beale butchered two Scots pine trees. This added light - worth £40,579 – to the value of his property. He was ordered to yield that sum, on top of a fine.†

Nature was the victim of these criminal acts. But the home owners were not allowed to pocket the Rent that reflected the value of nature.

* Izzy Ferris (2019), "Millionaire fined £170k for illegally axing 11 trees", *Daily Mail*, April 12.
† *Daily Mail* (2019), "Fined £60,000, millionaire butchered trees to boost value of £1.2m home", September 28.

When a person dies and turns to dust, relatives mourn but the fate of humanity is not affected. The template personality is transmitted biologically and sociologically through the generations. To achieve that timespace outcome, however, Rent has to be continuously produced and invested in the template personality. If the production of Rent was interrupted, or if Rent was diverted away from the population's welfare, the assets that made up the template personality – psychological, biological and aesthetic – would atrophy. That is why Rent was assigned the protection of the sacred. Reverence expressed the consecrated contract with nature: dishonour the deal, and humanity and the Social Galaxy would not flourish. Communities could not countenance cheating. And yet, *Homo sapiens* could not have come into existence if our ancestors had failed to develop the capacity to defy nature.

The need to cheat nature

To fashion the template personality, early humans had to reconfigure the material resources they needed to experiment with new ways of personal being and of group living. They required a supporting infrastructure, the space within which they could mobilise the power they needed. With that power, they built the Social Galaxy that rotated within the universe as people adapted to new habitats and the social opportunities which they created for themselves.

None of this could have happened if they had not learnt how to create the power which gave them control over their destiny. But that unique power came at a price. It emerged solely because of a non-negotiable obligation, which was specified in an unwritten contract. The one life-or-death clause in the contract ruled that cheating could never be directed inwards into society. *Dishonour the contract, and the ensuing disorder - entropy - would destroy humanity.*

Entropy provides the clue as to why nature had to be manipulated. Through trial and error, early humans discovered one of nature's secrets: the 2nd Law of Thermodynamics. They worked out the impact of that law. This enabled them to trick the unremitting laws which orchestrate the forces of the universe. Armed with that knowledge, they clawed their way out of the clutches of the gravity that anchored other forms of life – animal and vegetable – to planet Earth.

Box 1.2 **The Rent of Society**

Individuals working together create Rent when resources are invested in the social services and infrastructure that they need. Those investments are self-funding, as was illustrated by the £3.4bn invested in the extension of London's Jubilee underground railway. New tracks were laid from Waterloo Station along the south bank of the Thames to the Canary Wharf financial district.

Don Riley, a commercial property owner, was intrigued by the rise in the value of his properties that were located near two of the Jubilee stations. Rents rose even before the trains had begun to roll! When he investigated, he found that the sale value of sites clustered around ten stations had risen by more than £13bn. This was solely due to the provision of public transport.[*]

Offsetting such transport-related gains are losses from living near highways. Motor vehicles emit killer levels of carbon. Residents in some of those locations can suffer acute respiratory failure leading to death. Ella Kissi-Debrah, who lived 80ft from a busy highway in South London, was one victim.[†] That is one reason why heavily polluted locations register lower Rent values.

[*] Fred Harrison (2006), *Wheels of Fortune*, Ch.3. iea.org
[†] Phoebe Southworth (2019), "New inquest to investigate if air pollution killed girl, 9", *Daily Telegraph*, May 3.

Physicists apply mathematics and the theories of quantum mechanics to develop a granular portrait of spacetime in nature. Our ancestors had to rely on intuition to understand how the 2nd Law is a process whereby energy is defused and decomposed as it moves from hot to cold forms; from a state of order to disorder. Flowers consume energy from the sun: as they bask in the rays, the heat dissipates. The decomposed granules of energy are rendered unusable. There is no way for a flower to reuse the energy it has absorbed from the sun.

A stone club, an iron axe and an iPhone have one thing in common: they do not have infinite lives. Materials decay at a

---

Box 1.3 **The composite value of Rent**

Rent that people offer to pay for residential and commercial locations are a composite value of the services of both nature and society, as illustrated by the network of canals in Britain.

Waterways were constructed at the end of the 18th century, just before the onset of the railway age. They were designed to move heavy goods in the first decades of the Industrial Revolution. Today, canals are valued for the aesthetic benefits that enrich life. People are willing to pay a premium for the right to live close to flowing water, so that they can look at the reeds bending in the wind.

Researchers at the London School of Economics measured the premium on properties across England and Wales. On average, a buyer paid 3-4% more for a property within 100m of a canal relative to prices elsewhere (in 2016 prices). This premium fell to zero beyond 100m.[*]

The premium is higher in dense urban areas, where green space is scarce. Savills, the London real estate agency, calculated that a premium of 36.7% is paid for locations within 160 feet of a park in Hampstead and Highgate.[†]

[*] LSE Centre for Economic Performance (2019), "Valuing the environmental benefits of canals using house prices", spatial-economics.blogspot.com
[†] "Price of Living near Green Space", *Daily Telegraph*, May 18, 2019.

rate prescribed by the 2ⁿᵈ Law. In the language of economics, they depreciate. To maintain their productivity, assets have to be renewed. This requires a steady flow of new resources for investment in assets that help people to maintain their standard of living.

Our pre-historical ancestors did not need to know that the 1ˢᵗ Law of Thermodynamics (also known as the Law of Conservation of Energy), states that energy cannot be created or destroyed. But they *did* need to understand that energy changes its composition. The direction of travel – from order to disorder – is irreversible. It is the overwhelming obstacle to the evolution of self-consciousness and complex communities. For sentient life to achieve awareness of itself and its environs, a sustained state of order is needed. That was one of the accomplishments of early humans. For them, the past was not a dead space; the future was not a blank vacuum. But this order could only be achieved by postponing the dynamic effects of the 2ⁿᵈ Law. A technique was needed to trick nature, so that its power could be harnessed to create something unique in the universe.

This need was not confined to chipping flint stones to create stone axes. The techniques of accumulation were pivotal to the evolution of the psychology and physiology of human beings, as well as in material objects which could be used and reused as tools. To achieve this feat, energy had to be reconstituted into two forms: soft power and hard power.

Soft power was needed to shape the template personality. This necessitated the evolution of the brain with the capacity to reason; and the reshaping of the jaw so that sounds could be converted into the words that enriched the capacity to communicate. That is how the first anatomically modern humans, the Cro-Magnon, came to learn how to mimic the laws of nature. They achieved this so that they could extract resources for investment in the legacy assets, which had to include the codes of conduct which disciplined the behaviour of thinking people. Anthropologist Paul Radin stressed that the codes were "based upon behaviour. No mere enunciation of an ideal of love, no matter how often and sincerely repeated, would gain an individual...admiration, sympathy, or respect. Every ethical precept must be submitted to the touchstone of conduct".[1] The codes were the pillars of the covenant that sealed communities into viable systems and rendered people fit to adapt their way into a unique place on Earth.[2] The more complex the innovations, the richer the fabric of people's lives.

▶ *At the individual level*, spiritual sensibilities nurtured sentiments which included empathy and reciprocity. These mental adaptations made it possible to extend cooperative activity and enhance economic productivity above the levels that could be achieved by other species.

Primatologist Frans de Wall observed how cooperation operated in other species: "If one hyena or pelican...monopolise[d] all rewards, the system would collapse. Survival depends on sharing, which explains why both humans and animals are exquisitely sensitive to fair divisions...chimpanzees and humans go even further by moderating their share of joint rewards to prevent frustration of others. We owe our sense of fairness to a long history of mutualistic cooperation".[3] Humans did synchronise their behaviour to operate with the grain of nature, but also with the grain of the laws that drove the Social Galaxy, which gave them the power to negotiate the contract with nature (Box 1.4).

1. Paul Radin (1927), *Primitive Man as Philosopher*; New York: New York Review of Books (2017), p.71
2. Marcia Pally (2017), "More than a resource: covenant as a basis for societal organiza-tion", in Torsten Meireis and Rolf Schieder (Eds.), *Religion and Democracy*. http://www.nomos-shop.de/_assets/downloads/9783848741359_lese01.pdf
3. Frans de Wall (2014), "Why Humans and Other Primates Cooperate", *Scientific American*. https://nickrath.weebly.com/uploads/6/5/4/1/6541061/why_humans_and_other_primates_cooperate_-_scientific_american.pdf

---

Box 1.4 **Are humans exceptional?**

My claim that humans are exceptional will be contested. In the past, the uniqueness of humans was based on inferences from anatomical evidence. Nonsense, concludes Niccolo Caldararo of San Francisco State University, after reviewing the physiological case. And as for human use of tools, he notes that beavers build dams and birds build nests. Bees even have language.* Therefore, "humans are no more unique than (*sic*) other animals and that we fit in to a series of variations in the animal world (both living and dead) that becomes apparent the more one knows about comparative physiology and behaviour".†

What distinguishes humans from all the other species is the capacity to defy the 2nd Law of Thermodynamics. Tools employed by other species are picked up and, after use, are discarded. They are not "produced". Humans refashion materials to make them reusable for years to come. In doing so, their labour and investments defy the process of entropy.

* R. Chavin (1965), *Animal Societies from Bee to Gorilla*, London: Hill and Wang.
† Niccolo Caldararo (2009), "The Tendency to make Man an Exception", *Primatology: Theories, Methods and Research* (eds: E. Potocki and J. Krasinski), Nova Science Publishers, p.122.

▶ *At the institutional level*, practices were devised that provided the capacity to administer complex forms of spiritual and secular organisations. These enabled the Social Galaxy to function in harmony with the natural universe.

These assets were transmitted between generations. But intergenerational bequests required the services of an operating mechanism that continuously affirmed the symbiotic relationship between people. The laws of land tenure served as the core elements of the covenant that established the spatial domain. They defined the territorial boundaries between individual and group rights of access to nature, and protected the interests of future generations. The rights of tenure came with the responsibility for transferring the Rent of the occupied land to the pool of common resources.

The Laws of Society

The evolution of self-consciousness brought with it the greatest of dangers, in the form of an attitude that could threaten the existence of humanity itself.

The wealth that people accumulated became the treasure trove that might be coveted by individuals with selfish interests at heart. To secure the continued evolution of the species, strategies were needed to protect that wealth, the legacy assets that defined humanity. There were two phases to the evolution of the techniques that were designed to defeat cheating.

In communities constructed around gathering and hunting, the greatest risk stemmed from the temptation to let others work to bring food to one's hearth. Why not let others take the risks of killing wild animals for the meat which would be brought back to the camp? Why dig the dirt oneself to extract the roots that would be turned into succulent meals in the cooking pot? Why not remain at home, in comfort and security, and then share in the spoils of other people's labour? That would be a nice life! *But it was not fair!*

There was an existential component to this cheating. If too many people sat back and indulged themselves in the ploys of living off the labours of others, there would come a point at which the resources that were shared in common – the legacy assets – would begin to depreciate faster than they were being repaired or replaced. That would throw the evolutionary process into reverse. Such a disengagement from the production of the Rent that was needed to compensate for nature's 2nd Law would be fatal to the existence of the evolutionary project.

Unwillingness to "pull one's weight" *had* to be censured. This took the form of personal interventions to ensure the balanced growth of communities through time. The existential importance of these interventions stemmed from the way they protected the core values of humanity. Those values (soft power) included respect for other people's needs, and the sense of fair play. They were the psychological coagulants that enabled individuals to evolve into co-operative groups, the nucleus of which was the extended family. Values were supplemented with emotions that solidified relationships. Words like *empathy* and *reciprocity* reveal the human condition at its warmest: the creation and extension of human energy as individuals participated in communal activities and shared themselves and the products of their labours with others. This behaviour included the bequest of personal resources for the welfare of those who were in need of support.[4] The primordial values and sentiments were transmitted through the generations to find their expression in sacred texts (Box 1.5).

Hard power also had to be protected. This evolved in the form of the technologies that helped people to produce the goods and services they needed. As horizons of the mind expanded, so production with the aid of increasingly sophisticated tools was extended from stone implements to objects fashioned with the aid of fire. Knowledge of how to produce and renew these aids became part of the legacy assets that were gifted between the generations.

As dreams were transformed into reality, the interventions against cheating had to be routinised. By developing these techniques, humanity moved inexorably onto an evolutionary pathway that would one day enable people to walk on the moon.

---

4. Neanderthals, the cousins of prehistoric humans, have revealed the scale of the generosity towards those in need. Archaeologist Penny Spikins has described the condition of 50 skeletons: one in three displayed signs of serious injury or illness. Some were disabled for many years, which meant they had to be cared for by other members of their groups. Sarah Knapton (2019), "Museums urged to display the harsh realities of Neanderthal lives", *Daily Telegraph*, September 13. https://www.telegraph.co.uk

---

Box 1.5 **Empathy as the Golden Rule**

In an anthology complied by Robert Runcie (Archbishop of Canterbury [1980-1991]) and Basil Hume (Archbishop of Westminster [1976-1999]), empathy is shown to be a guiding principle of all the faiths. Judaism expresses it in these emphatic terms: "What is hateful to you, do not to your fellow men. That is the entire Law; all the rest is commentary". In Christianity: "Whatever you wish that men would do to you, do so to them; for this is the law and the prophets." In islam: "No one of you is a believer until he desires for his brother that which he desires for himself". Similar strictures appear in the faiths ranging from Hinduism, Jainism Sikhism, Baha'i, Buddhism, Taoism and Zaroastrianism. In Confucianism, what philosophers call the "golden rule" is expressed in these terms: "Surely it is a maxim of loving-kindness: do not to others that which you would not have them do to you".*

* *Prayers for Peace* (1987), London: SPCK, p.98.

Teasing was effective in securing responsible behaviour between neighbours. The kinetic power of words was deployed to cause shame for more serious deeds. For transgressions regarded as beyond resolution, ostracism was the ultimate sanction. Being banished into the wilderness was as good as a death sentence. These strategies secured social cohesion. Offenders, suitably chastised, would back down and meet their personal responsibilities. The "considerable evolutionary pressure for detecting cheating"[5] resulted in the emergence of the techniques of discipline as a sociogenic necessity.[6] Personal interventions and admonitions prevented isolated acts from morphing into organised behaviour

---

5. Robert Sapolsky (2017), *Behave: The Biology of Humans at Our Best and Worst*, London: Vintage, p.324.
6. I formulated the sociogenic concept to distinguish my theory – of evolution driven by the social group – from the notion of evolution as driven by individual behaviour emphasised by E.O. Wilson in his *Sociobiology: The New Synthesis* (1975), Cambridge: Harvard University Press. See *The Traumatised Society* (2012), London: Shepheard-Walwyn, p.xiii.

that could rupture the solidarity on which everyone depended for survival.

Accounting for honest dealing

In urban-based civilisations, personal interventions were not sufficient to enforce appropriate behaviour on large concentrations of people. New rules and institutions had to be devised and enforced, albeit grounded in ancient wisdoms.

Some 10,000 years ago, in the first agricultural revolution, people accelerated the accumulation of resources and designed larger settlements. The personal interventions that maintained good order in earlier communities were now largely redundant.

New techniques were needed that reflected the complexities of civilisations which flourished along rivers like the Nile, the Tiber and the Euphrates.

The shift in the scale of living required more intensive forms of administration, including changes to tenure rights to land. When people learnt how to enhance productivity by planting seeds in the soil, they needed to settle on clearly defined plots of land. The investment of labour in land could only be recovered over a period of years. Urbanised communities also needed more complex systems of spirituality and authority, and the provision of large-scale infrastructure (such as the networks of canals that could deliver water to arid fields). To accommodate the new way of life, culture had to be enriched with three innovations.

1. *A social process* was required to ensure that the moral rules worked with the grain of nature across extensive spaces and lengthy time periods.

2. *Authority structures* were needed to enforce discipline and to deal with deviant behaviour, so that new horizons could be safely traversed.

3. *Defensive systems* were needed to protect the territory from external marauders who might be attracted by the visible increase in wealth.[7]

Urbanisation was the catalyst that enabled people to replicate in new surroundings the arrangements which they had created in their bid to emerge out of nature. They were able to experiment with institutions for organising their inter-personal relationships on terms which honoured values such as honesty and reciprocity. But further progress would not have been possible if they had failed to reaffirm that the net resources which they produced were the common property of their communities. To facilitate progress, they had to develop a pricing mechanism. This was needed because the duty to ensure the provision of the social infrastructure fell on the priests and princes. To fulfil that duty, they needed new techniques for measuring and securing the correct use of Rent.

The embryonic pricing system in antiquity emerged from the allocation of land to support those who administered the spiritual and political needs of the population. Priests and princes would not have the time to also work the land, so people devoted part of their labour time to working the fields that funded the temples and the palaces.

The earliest farmers needed to track the production and exchange of their produce. Archaeologist Denise Schmandt-Besserat has shown how tokens were invented to quantify grain and animals. Sophisticated symbols were needed to monitor the production and accumulation of resources. The logistical challenges became the incentive to invent numbers. These assumed a rich variety of forms in Egypt and Mesopotamia. As interpreted by Gordon Childe, and confirmed by subsequent generations of

7. Martin Hinsch and Jan Komdeur (2010), "Defence, intrusion and the evolutionary stability of territoriality", *J of Theoretical Biology*, Vol 266(4). Joan E. Strassmann and David C. Queller (2014), "Privatization and property in biology", *Animal Behaviour*, 92.

Assyriologists, numbers were invented before the symbols that represent the spoken word. Numbers served two purposes.

1. *Auditing the quantity and tracking the flow of Rent* from the fields to the grain stores in the temples or palaces.

The tracking technique ensured that farmers contributed to the services they shared in common. These ranged from infrastructure such as highways and waterways to the services delivered by the spiritual, political and intellectual members of these communities.

2. *Holding power to account*, to ensure that those to whom Rent had been entrusted used that value for the intended purposes.

The capacity to audit behaviour was needed to ensure that Rent was invested for the security and flourishing of the community. Numbers were the tools that delivered the transparency which disciplined the exercise of power.

Custodianship of the commons was made transparent by the accounts. No matter how revered were the priests or princes, as stewards they were accountable for what happened to the net income that was dedicated to funding their public offices.

The moral compass

Our narrative of the evolution of humanity can be tested scientifically. We can employ the tools of anthropology, archaeology and biology to interrogate the key elements of the organic system that guided the behaviour of our earliest ancestors. Crucial to this system was the concept of co-operation. Was this a universal characteristic, integral to cultures at all times and in all places where people lived?

Three Oxford anthropologists tested the proposition that the function of morality was to promote complex forms of cooperation. To interrogate the theory of "morality-as-coopera-tion" they compared the ethnographic records of 60 societies, which were radically different in their locations and cultures. The theory predicts behaviour as it relates to the regulation of relationships and to the allocation and use of nature's resources. The seven components of that behaviour are listed in Table 1.1. A consistent pattern emerged.

Table 1.1. **Universal moral rules**

1	Help your group: empathy
2	Return favours: reciprocity
3	Be brave
4	Defer to elders
5	Respect, obedience, loyalty
6	Divide disputed resources
7	Respect others' property

[T]he majority of these cooperative morals are observed in the majority of cultures, with equal frequency across all regions of the world. We conclude that these seven cooperative behaviours are plausible candidates for universal moral rules, and that morality-as-co-operation could provide the unified theory of morality that anthropology has hitherto lacked.[8]

These seven norms delivered stable inter-personal relation-ships, social cohesion and the flow of resources that facilitated the evolution of humans out of nature. Oliver Scott Curry and his Oxford colleagues explain that the obverse characteristics of

8. Oliver Scott Curry *et al* (2019), "Is It Good to Cooperate? Testing the Theory of Morality-as-Cooperation in 60 Societies", *Current Anthropology*, 60 (1).

the seven morally-sanctioned forms of behaviour are censured as morally unacceptable. These would include, for example, disrespect for others; free riding; unfairness; theft and neglect of kin.

The results of the fieldwork of generations of anthropologists and laboratory experiments by behavioural psychologists support my thesis: Rent, as the measure of the energy that was produced to be shared for the common good, underpinned the evolution of humanity.

Alternative theses

Perspectives that do not fit with my narrative have been developed. One of these is offered by Jared Diamond, a professor of geography who was ranked ninth in a poll of the world's top 100 public intellectuals.[9] He has written extensively on the collapse of civilisations, and he warns that we should not "romanticize traditional village living arrangements". It was in those settings that people were able to enforce social conventions through close and constant personal contact. But Diamond characterises these communities as living "like somewhat glorified chimpanzees".[10]

Those "glorified chimpanzees" were the architects of a sophisticated spatial realm that operated with laws that were invented by our ancient ancestors. Their customs and practices created a unique galaxy in the universe. This was achieved by preventing free riding from emerging to threaten the existence of the Social Galaxy. That form of cheating, if it had been allowed to mutate into a fully-formed culture, would have pushed people off the evolutionary trajectory on which they had embarked.

We all possess the template personality which early humans constructed. That means we are all capable of behaving decently,

---

9. https://en.wikipedia.org/wiki/Jared_Diamond
10. Jared Diamond (2019), "What we gain or lose in cities", *National Geographic*, April, pp.17-18.

notwithstanding the pressures to act selfishly. But behaviour is not deterministically fixed to produce only the good things in life. Actual outcomes are the consequence of the combination of influences which include those emanating from the cultural *milieu*. Biology, the legacy assets and our individual personalities are mixed into a cocktail of self-consciousness. One possible outcome is anti-social behaviour. The spectrum of such behaviour begins with low-grade cheating and may gravitate all the way to taking orders from a Hitler to gas people in ovens. That is why it is incumbent on all of us to remain alert to the flaws in the human personality, like the temptation to indulge in free riding. Because once mainstream culture has been polluted, it could end in catastrophe. It has happened before.

Ancient history reveals the abuses that blight the human record. Michael Hudson, an economic analyst who began his career in Wall Street before turning his attention to the finances of Babylon, summarised the origins of some of those episodes by noting that

> Throughout antiquity there was a tendency for the wealthiest families, above all the landed aristocracy, to break free of fiscal obligations. This threw the tax burden onto the shoulders of the classes least able to bear them, culminating in a fiscal crisis that smothered further economic development.[11]

Because the implications of those episodes in antiquity have been forgotten, our world now faces the severest of existential threats. To aid us in avoiding the collapse into another Dark Age, we need a theory of everything that lays bare the evolutionary dynamics of the Social Galaxy. Scientists are searching for such a theory of the universe. General relativity (which focuses on gravity), and quantum field theory (which focuses on sub-atomic particles, atoms and molecules) are in contention.

---

11. Michael Hudson (2000), "Mesopotamia and Classical Antiquity", in R.V. Andelson (ed.), *Land-Value Taxation Around the World*, 3rd edn., Oxford: Blackwell, p.7.

To complement the physics of the material universe we need a metaphysics of Rent if we are to restore the Social Galaxy back on the path of evolution.

Rent integrates the biological, psychological and social dimensions of humanity. For good or bad, it will determine the fate of our species. Rent successfully served as the organising mechanism for humans who occupied an intimate niche in nature, but could it also sustain the Social Galaxy once humans had transformed the geology of the planet into the new age which is now called the Anthropocene?

CHAPTER TWO

The Science of Good Governance

Humans did not evolve by accident. Under nature's laws, entropy dissolves energy. So in the natural course of events, *Homo sapiens* ought never to have come into existence. But early humans applied labour power in a way that defeated the laws of nature. The trick was to crystallise energy in a complex combination of assets – biological, psychological and social.

Pre-modern people learnt how to plan. This enabled them to devise strategies to offset nature's process of wear and tear. They discovered how to renew the assets they inherited from previous generations. Growth by small, incremental steps was in the favoured direction. This evolutionary process was contingent on the willingness to continuously produce a stream of net resources – Rent – that could be invested in the fabric of their being.

Why, then, are we locked into a chaos that threatens us, and other species, with descent into extinction? Is it because we have not learnt how to adapt evolutionary principles to organisationally complex modern technologies? Are we estranged from the skills and knowledge that originally led to the formation of *Homo sapiens*? The answer is a straightforward No! We have at our disposal, spelt out in scientific language, the paradigm which defined the terms for the growth of our self-sustaining species.

The core of that model is the distinction between the flow of energy called Rent, and the energy that has to be consumed on a daily basis to ensure biological survival.

Once our species had matured, Rent was intentionally assigned the protection of spiritual attributes, accorded sacred status in ways that sustained early humans along the evolutionary pathway.

▶ *Spirituality*: part of the net produce, some of it in the form of labour time, was devoted to sacred activities:
  – supporting holy men who administered to people's mental wellbeing;
  – funding the ritual activities that bonded communities; and
  – constructing sacred sites where nature could be thanked for its riches.

▶ *Reverence*: resources devoted to the aesthetic activities that inspired the imagination, beyond the realm of the profane:
  – art: to awaken the wonderment of life beyond the material;
  – music: to elevate the spirit and enrich social solidarity; and
  – dance: to integrate people into symbolic associations.

▶ *Devotion*: activities that affirmed realities beyond what could be selfishly appropriated or comprehended:
  – ancestors were worshipped, to demonstrate gratitude for past labours that gave them sentient life;
  – the willingness to risk one's self to save those in danger, acknowledging the sacred nature of life; and
  – aiding those in need, including animals, to affirm the virtue of the spirit of co-operation.

Those values made it possible for the Social Galaxy to function in dynamic equilibrium. The system built the power of self-propulsion, guided by people's aspirations and emerging capacities. To sustain that momentum, energy had to be continuously added to the legacy assets that were transmitted to the next generation. Reduction in that quantum of net energy meant regression, the retreat to chaos, yielding to nature's law of entropy. That is why free riding *had* to be suppressed.

Cheating, if it was allowed to gain traction as an acceptable form of behaviour, would coalesce into an intrusive culture. If that happened, the corrosive impact would manifest itself in the depletion of the capacity of the Social Galaxy to function. Energy would be drained away from the legacy assets that constituted humanity.

Urbanisation brought with it the need for hierarchies of decision-making. Benefits from the stratification of populations included the creation of role models, the provision of dispute resolution, a division of labour and, notes one sociologist, "the collective punishment of free-riders".[1]

Three benchmarks were recognised as necessary to secure the health of communities.

1. The obligation to work to fund the reproduction of the population.

2. Agreement to renew the pooled legacy assets ("the commons").

3. Cherishing the universe, from the stars in the heavens to the roots buried in the soil.

There were traps and trials along the way. But the evolutionary blueprint was built into the living tissue that became humanity.

---

1. Tilman Hartley (2019), "The continuing evolution of ownership", PLOS One, p.5. https://doi.org/10.1371/journal.pone.0211871

At first, early humans relied on intuition for their understanding of that blueprint. It took 3,000 years of philosophising for the formula to be expressed in scientific language, in terms that were consistent with both ancient moral codes and the laws of nature.

The Single Tax

Philosophers in France formulated the basic principles for the science of good governance. They explained that it was neither necessary nor desirable to tax wages, because to do so damaged people's welfare. Similar distortions occurred when government taxed consumption goods, or placed tariffs on cross-border trade. Disruptions to the economy and society occurred because taxes on people's earned incomes increased the price of goods traded in the marketplace. This had regressive effects (the quality of life of low-income families was reduced). And it tempted investors to divert their capital to less efficient uses, which nonetheless left them better off because they avoided the payment of taxes.

The Physiocrats, as they were known, identified the nation's net income – Rent – as the efficient source of revenue to fund the services provided by the State.

Adam Smith, a professor of moral philosophy in Glasgow, heard about the Single Tax. He travelled to Paris to study at first-hand the details of the model for funding public services. The outcome was a seminal work of scholarship which laid the foundations for economics as a social science. In *The Wealth of Nations*, published in 1776, he made it clear that government should fund its services by collecting what he called Ground Rent.

Smith's genius was to articulate a new model not just of governance, but of society. The whole edifice rested on three pillars. First, he opposed the protectionist policy pursued by the UK in international trade. Mercantilism, as it was called, reduced the wealth of the nation. Second, Smith realised that, to move society

Adam Smith travelled to Paris to study at first-hand the details of the model for funding public services.

beyond the feudal model, the vast landed estates of the Crown had to be transferred into the hands of people who could put those tracts to productive use. In doing so, huge benefits would accrue to the nation, creating new forms of employment and expanding the opportunities that were emerging in the urban sector.[2] A new model of society was needed, one that responded to the opportunities that were emerging through industrialisation. The third pillar was the efficient collection of revenue by government.

Adam Smith's triadic model provided the blueprint for inclusive prosperity. Within it,

- ► individuals acted responsibly, covering the costs of goods and services provided by the public and private sectors;

- ► the State desisted from taxes that damaged people's wealth and health and funded social infrastructure out of Rent; and

- ► society was integrated with the aid of a pricing mechanism that deterred anti-social behaviour like tax-dodging.

---

2. Adam Smith (1776), *The Wealth of Nations*, Bk 5, Ch 2, Pt. 2, p.348. Page references are to the edition edited by Edwin Cannan (1976), Chicago: University of Chicago Press.

This arrangement accorded with the principles of proportionality: the prices charged in both the private and public sectors were symmetrically related to the costs of the goods and services provided either by entrepreneurs or the state. This ensured the efficient allocation of resources, which optimised wealth; and it honoured the moral codes, which maximised people's well-being.

Given such an arrangement, an individual was liberated to pursue personal interests while simultaneously he "necessarily labours to render the annual revenue of the society as great as he can". This was achieved because the social framework was the "invisible hand". Now, people could go about the business of fulfilling their daily needs and aspirations while – by fulfilling their social responsibilities through the payment of Rent into the public purse – honouring the interests of everyone else.[3]

If this model had been adopted, the outcome would have systematically erased the cheating behaviour that had emerged over the previous 200 years in the form of free riding. This would have yielded an inclusive industrialised society that liberated the individual while disciplining governance. The pricing system would have integrated the working population with the political process into a harmonious partnership.

The key was the doctrine of the Single Tax. Rent, as humanity's operating mechanism, met the tests of both justice and economic efficiency. People would be free to possess and exchange land according to their needs, and government would collect the Ground Rent to fund public services such as education and provide those public highways that were beyond the means of the private sector. In *The Wealth of Nations*, Smith affirmed the logic of revenue from Ground Rent. After all, he pointed out, Ground Rents…

---

3. *The Wealth of Nations*, Bk 4, Ch 2; p.477.

are altogether owing to the good government of the sovereign, which, by protecting the industry either of the whole people, or of the inhabitants of some particular place, enables them to pay so much more than its real value for the ground which they build their houses upon...Nothing can be more reasonable than that a fund which owes its existence to the good government of the state, should be taxed peculiarly.[4]

Under this model, government would work with the grain of the factory-based economy that was emerging in the final quarter of the 18th century. The outcome would have been qualitatively different from the one that offended the sensibilities of Karl Marx.[5] Adam Smith's Ground Rent would have empowered the industrial revolutionists of the British Isles to chart new pathways to a prosperity that would have enriched everyone, including the offspring of the peasants who had been rudely deprived of their traditional right of access to the commons. This classical system was based on the smooth integration of the three factors of production (Fig. 2.1).

The classical model provided an elegant diagnostic framework for allocating income. Government could identify the Ground Rent which provided an accurate measure of the annual value of the combined services of nature and society at each location. That eliminated the need to tax wages or the profits of entrepreneurship. The practical outcome was the freedom to allocate resources in efficient proportions to produce optimum personal gratification in the course of fulfilling one's social responsibilities. No-one was excluded from their share of the benefits that accrued from working for a living.

---

4. *The Wealth of Nations*; Bk 5, Ch 2, Pt 2, Art 1, p.371.
5. Marx, when he wrote the *Communist Manifesto* with Frederick Engels, did place the socialisation of Rent at the top of his 10 demands. But he was not able to visualise how that would be sufficient to create the platform for the inclusive freedoms that would empower people to calibrate the industrial economy on new relationships between the owners of capital and the owners of labour. So he chose to locate all productive resources under the control of a centralised command, which he chose to called the "dictatorship of the proletariat".

Figure 2.1 **The classical model of the economy**

Adam Smith's model was not complete. A deeper account was needed of the spatial component of the economy. The missing piece was recorded by David Ricardo, an English stockbroker-turned-politician, in *Principles of Political Economy and Taxation* (1817).

Ricardo described how the mobility of labour and capital had the effect of equalising wages and profits across the economy. If wages were higher in one location than elsewhere, people had the option of migrating to take advantage of the better opportunities. This tended to equalise wages within each sector of production across the economic catchment area. The same thing happened with capital. If the returns on savings and investments were less than elsewhere, these assets could be reallocated to take advantage of higher profits. This would equalise the returns in the capital markets. The propensity to move is known as the *elasticity* of labour and capital. The concept evokes the fluidity with which people and their savings could shift between locations or into new activities.

The land market conformed to different principles. Land (in its urban or agricultural forms) was immobile, or *inelastic*. The supply is fixed by nature, physically anchored in place within the economic catchment area.[6] Mobility, therefore, cannot equalise Rent across an economic space. Plots of urban land cannot be transported from towns of relatively low productivity to urban conurbations of high productivity which yield higher Rents. Fertile farmland cannot be relocated closer to urban consumers (thereby incurring lower transport costs for the delivery of products to consumers).

Locations at the furthest point from the centres of activity were termed by Ricardo as marginal. At the margin, people could occupy land and earn their living, but they would have nothing left to pay as Rent. The theory is schematically illustrated in Figure 2.2.

Figure 2.2 **Ricardian rent based locations**

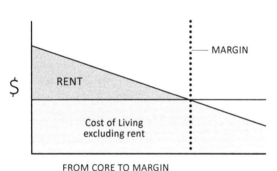

6. Singapore has expanded its land mass by almost 25% by importing sand to extend its territorial size. The revenue produced on such locations should correctly be divided between Rent and profits, since capital is embedded in the extension of the city state into the Pacific. With the depreciation of the capital investment in those extensions, however, eventually the net revenue would be exclusively Rent.

Beyond the margin, total output drops below what is needed to cover the costs of labour and capital, let alone generate Rent. In these sub-marginal areas, land is left to the birds and the bees.

Ricardo's law of Rent was not an artificial construct, or peculiar to modern times. Ancient civilisations conformed to these principles of production. This may be observed in the productivity of plots of land along the banks of the canals that brought water to the arid soils of Mesopotamia. Drawing on information retrieved from clay tablets, Assyriologists discovered that the value of land (as measured in silver) was a function of its productivity, which was determined by the soil's fertility and proximity to water.[7] Fields located closest to the canal were the most productive, so they delivered higher Rents! It is now possible to compare the data from the third millennium BC with the operations of a modern land market like Australia's.[8]

In the 20th century, economists applied maths to test the theory. They confirmed that Rent was the fiscally optimal method for raising revenue. Joseph Stiglitz and his co-author Anthony Atkinson emphasised the social significance of Rent in their textbook. This policy, they wrote,

> ...has been dubbed the 'Henry George' theorem, since not only is the land tax non-distortionary, but also it is the 'single tax' required to finance the public good.[9]

Post-classical economists, however, debase the nature of Rent. They detach the concept from its evolutionary roots. In the 19th century, some authors like utilitarian philosopher John Stuart Mill did include the classical treatment of Rent in their discourses,

7. Ignace J. Gelb et al (1991), Earliest Land Tenure Systems in the Near East-Ancient Kudurrus, Oriental Institute of the University of Chicago, Vol. 104, p.283.
8. Cameron K. Murray (2019), Marginal and average prices of land lots should not be equal: A critique of Glaeser and Gyourko's method for identifying residential price effects of town planning regulations, pp.19-20. https://papers.ssrn.com/sol3/papers.cfm?abstract_id=3328308
9. Anthony B. Atkinson and Joseph E. Stiglitz (1980), Lectures on Public Economics, London: McGraw-Hill, p.585.

but they did not explore the profound social, psychological and ecological implications. The one major exception was Henry George, an American journalist.

George was puzzled by the extensive poverty in a continent that was rich in natural resources. He addressed that issue in *Progress and Poverty*. He traced personal, communal and environmental crises to the way governments raised their revenue. And he identified the tax regime as a product of the history in which the commons had been appropriated by people who set themselves up as landlords.

In *Progress and Poverty* Henry George explained the high incidence of poverty amidst plenty.

By translating classical theory into popular language, George was able to reach a mass audience which turned itself into the first global reform movement. Einstein became one of his admirers (Box 2.1). George emphasised that problems like poverty were not attributable to "market failure": the market would operate on benign terms, if people were not hindered from acting in their best interests. Good governance would not impose the psycho-social traumas that ruptured people's lives. But this rosy prospectus depended on one condition: *the re-socialisation of Rent and the privatisation of people's earned incomes*.[10]

---

10. Henry George (1879), *Progress and Poverty*; 1979, centenary edition, New York: Robert Schalkenbach Foundation.

Box 2.1 **Einstein's verdict**

In a letter to Henry George's daughter, Anna George DeMille, Albert Einstein wrote:

I have already read Henry George's great book and really learnt a great deal from it. Yesterday evening I read with admiration the address about Moses. Men like Henry George are rare unfortunately. One cannot imagine a more beautiful combination of intellectual keenness, artistic form and fervent love of justice. Every line is written as if for our generation. The spreading of these works is a really deserving cause, for our generation especially has many and important things to learn from Henry George.*

* Albert Einstein letter, published in the May-June 1934 issue of *Land and Freedom*. http://www.cooperative-individualism.org/einstein-albert_henry-george-and-his-principles-1934.htm

---

The Free Riding Model

Between the 16th and 18th centuries, Rent had been converted into the anti-social instrument for privileging the power of the aristocracy and gentry. Because this flow of revenue was privatised, it inhabited an alien zone beyond the reach of those who worked to create it. In that anti-social arrangement, wages were only sufficient to sustain people's biological needs. Rent was no longer at the service of humanity. People were locked into a process which depleted those qualities that constituted the template personality. The evolutionary rules were abused by the free riders. Property rights and public finance became the Ugly Twin Sisters. Humane values were degraded to the status of Cinderella in the rent seeking system.

Adam Smith did not pull his punches…

As soon as the land of any country has all become private property, the landlords, like all other men, love to reap where they never sowed, and demand a rent even for its natural produce. The wood of the forest, the grass of the field, and all the natural fruits of the earth, which, when land was in common, cost the labourer only the trouble of gathering them, come, even to him, to have an additional price fixed upon them. He must then pay for the licence to gather them; and must give up to the landlord a portion of what his labour either collects or produces. This portion, or, what comes to the same thing, the price of this portion, constitutes the rent of land.[11]

He wrote that "To gratify the most childish vanity was the sole motive of the great proprietors" who

As soon…as they could find a method of consuming the whole value of their rents themselves, they had no disposition to share them with any other persons. For a pair of diamond buckles perhaps, or for something as frivolous and useless, they exchanged the maintenance, or what is the same thing, the price of the maintenance of a thousand men for a year…The buckles, however, were to be all their own, and no other human creature was to have any share of them.[12]

As for their role as administrators of the kingdom, Smith was equally scathing.

They are, indeed, too often defective in this tolerable knowledge. They are the only one of the three orders whose revenue costs them neither labour nor care, but comes to them, as it were, of its own accord, and independent of any plan or project of their own. That indolence, which is the natural effect of the ease and security of their situation, renders them too often, not only ignorant, but incapable of that application of mind which is necessary in order to foresee and understand the consequences of any public regulation.[13]

Smith displayed his contempt for the way the landed class devoted Rent to what is now called "conspicuous consumption", while merchants invested their money in productive enterprises.

---

11. *The Wealth of Nations*, Bk 1, Ch 6, p.56.
12. *The Wealth of Nations*, Bk 3, Ch 4; pp. 440, 437.
13. *The Wealth of Nations*, Bk 1, Ch 11; pp 276-277.

Thus did rent seeking triumph over value-adding in the body politic. To achieve this outcome, the alien culture relied on intrusive strategies that were designed to plunder the public purse by sluicing Rent into private pockets:

▶ *codes of conduct*: laws and morals were trimmed to accommodate the insatiable appetite of those living on Rent;

▶ *institutionalised power*: the rent seeking virus was transmitted through the professions and property markets; and

▶ *class relationships*: the hierarchical classification ensured that free riders remained in charge, atop everyone else.

Could it have been otherwise? Were the Physiocrats and Adam Smith whistling in the wind? Societies evolve by imagining better ways of living. And so it is with people in modern times. This is affirmed by what evolved within one country in Europe in the two centuries that followed the publication of *The Wealth of Nations*.

Denmark's Open Secret

Despite the efforts of the Physiocrats, the Single Tax was not applied in France. A serious attempt was made by Anne-Robert Turgot who, in 1774, was appointed Controller-General of Finances by Louis XVI. Turgot had worked in rural France as an administrator, and he had detected pre-revolutionary discontent in the population. That was why he prescribed the need to reform the state's finances.[14] But his attempt to introduce the Single Tax led to a conspiracy in court. No time was lost in ousting him from office. What chance France had of avoiding what turned into a bloody revolution went out of the door with Turgot.

14. A.R.J. Turgot (1770), *Reflections on the Formation and the Distribution of Riches*.

Might history have taken a different course if France, the leading culture of Europe, had applied the doctrine of the Single Tax? How confident can we be that social evolution would have been in a benign direction if Turgot's reform had been instituted? For answers we must turn to what was then one of the backwaters of the continent, to examine what happened in what Shakespeare called "the rotten state of Denmark".

Three turning points created modern Denmark.

▶ Late in the 18th century the king, Frederik VI, emancipated the serfs in a land-to-the-tiller programme. This was followed, early in the 19th century, by the hartkorn tax on manorial estates, which channelled more than half of Rents into the public purse.

▶ Recalling the bloody French Revolution, the Danes realised they needed a different route to democracy. A system of folk schools for adults was created across the country, which were established at the behest of poet-priest Nikolai Grundtvig.

▶ In the 1920s, responding to the publicity given to American social reformer Henry George, the land value tax was introduced, as championed by teachers in the folk schools. They triumphed over the objections of conservative reactionaries.[15]

Economically and socially, Denmark flourished. But then, in the 1960s, the share of revenue from the direct charge on Rent was diminished in response to the rise of conservative forces.[16]

---

15. An overview of this history is provided in "Revolution Danish Style, a YouTube video on the Geophilos channel: https://www.youtube.com/watch?v=J5_ I6noGOps
16. Ole Lefmann and Karsten K. Larsen (2000) "Denmark", in R.V. Andelson, *Land-Value Taxation Around the World*, 3rd edn., Oxford: Blackwell.

Figure 2.3 **European labour costs**

Private sector hourly rate (€) 2018

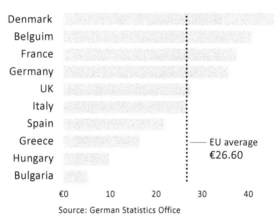

Source: German Statistics Office

Nonetheless, by then the social solidarity that was nurtured by the land-and-tax history was embedded in the people and institutions of Denmark.

This history falsifies the theories of post-classical economists like those identified as the Chicago School. They claim that governments which collect a high proportion of national income undermine the efficiency of the economy. That is how they justify the mantra of "small state/low taxes". On that basis, Denmark ought to be the least competitive economy in Europe and a most unhappy society. Because of the government's tax-take, it tops the list of hourly labour costs (Figure 2.3).

And yet, according to the OECD Better Life report, Danes enjoy a better work-life balance than any of the countries it surveyed.[1] Just 2% of employees regularly work very long hours, compared to the OECD average of 13%. Furthermore, Danes rank above average in a long list of areas: environmental quality,

---

1. http://www.oecdbetterlifeindex.org/countries/denmark/

civic engagement, education, skills, jobs, earnings, well-being and personal security. The metrics on social connections – the social support networks – is an important indicator of the fabric of communities: 96% of Danes report having friends or relatives they can count on in times of trouble, compared with 88% across other OECD countries.

But what about those high taxes? According to a Bloomberg report, Danes say they don't mind the tax take, because these fund their welfare, a public service which they treasure.[2] Their vigilance on how their money is spent is indicated by their level of engagement in politics: it exceeds the rate in most other OECD countries.

► Danes report the highest levels of life satisfaction of all countries surveyed by the OECD.

► The state of happiness is assessed in the World Happiness Report. Each year, Denmark vies for top place with Finland.

► On corruption, as measured by Transparency International's comparison of 180 countries in its Corruption Perceptions Index (2018), Denmark tops the list as the least corrupt nation in the world.

On education, 80% of adults aged 25-64 have completed upper-secondary education, which is four percentage points higher than the OECD average. On the metric of social mobility, Figure 2.4 reveals that it takes two generations for poorer Danish families to approach mean income (60 years). In the UK it takes five generations (150 years). In France and Germany, it takes six generations for poor families to work their way up to earning the mean income.

2. https://www.bloomberg.com/news/articles/2016-09-13/danes-loves-their-high-taxes

Figure 2.4 **The Mobility Gap**

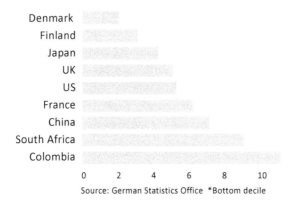

Generations it would take for descendants of poorer*
families to appraoc mean income

Source: German Statistics Office *Bottom decile

But did the burden of taxation prejudice the population's ability to generate material wealth as measured by gross domestic product (GDP)? Evidently not. According to the CIA's World Factbook, estimates based on purchasing power parity in 2017 recorded the Danes as having produced $50,100, marginally below the German performance ($50,800), and far ahead of France ($44,100) and the UK ($44,300).[3]

The exceptionalism of Denmark is thrown into sharp relief by comparisons with her neighbours.

► **France:** Something vital was missing from the revolutionary proclamation of "liberty, equality and fraternity". For despite experiments with five republics and constitutions over the following 200 years, in 2019 many citizens donned yellow vests to register their

---

3. https://www.cia.gov/library/publications/the-world-factbook/

Box 2.2 **The "crazy language" of politicians**

Holger Bech Nielsen is a Danish theoretical physicist and professor emeritus at the Niels Bohr Institute, at the University of Copenhagen. Among his achievements is his foundation work on "string theory", which seeks to offer an ultimate explanation for the physics of the universe. In his view, law-makers ought to conform to the disciplines of physics.

In *Teorien om alt* [*The Theory of Everything*], Nielsen's interrogator stated: "For the first time during the four years of the interviews for this book, the conversation about taxes on land and property gets Holger Bech Nielsen to exhibit something that can be interpreted as anger".*

Nielsen was angry because of the failure to tax land. "When you tax something, you reduce the desire for it, but it is harmless to tax land." He directed anger at the absurdity of the tax havens that encourage tax dodging. This behaviour, he observed, was encouraged by legislation drafted by law-makers in "crazy language".

* Holger Bech Nielsen and Jonas Kuld Rathje (2019), *Teorien om alt*, Copenhagen: Gyldendal, pp.113-114.

discontent with their government's tax plans. On one Saturday, the rioters wrecked dozens of shops in the Champs Elysees.

▶ **Germany:** Following World War 2, people enjoyed an exemplary housing market.[4] By 2019, the streets of Berlin were filled with demonstrators who, reported Reuters, vented anger over surging rents. The protesters demanded the expropriation of 200,000 apartments that had been sold to private landlords, which they said had changed the character of their city.[5]

4. John Muellbauer (1992) "Anglo-German Differences in Housing Market Dynamics: the Role of Institutions and Macro Economic Policy", *European Econ. Rev*. Papers and Proceedings 36.
5. Caroline Copley (2019), "Berlin activists march to demand city seize housing from landlords", April 6. reuters.com

▶ **Britain:** Brexit was one of the ingredients in a lethal
cocktail of public outrage at a state of affairs that had
disunited the kingdom. The epic scale of child poverty,
homelessness, mental ill-health and institutional failures
(to be documented in later chapters), suggests that there
is a fundamental flaw in the operating mechanisms of
the disunited kingdom.

By studying Denmark, we can derive profound historical and
sociological insights. And if there are problems in our world,
we ought to focus attention on the tax system according to a
distinguished physicist who, as it happens, is a Dane (Box 2.2).

If an alien culture has captured Europe's nation-states, this
outcome did not arise because the evolutionary principles that
guided humanity were lost in modern times. Those principles
were pushed aside. How this was achieved is revealed by what
happened in England.

CHAPTER THREE

Anatomy of a Captured State: England

England was exceptional. In the process of extending direct control over the British Isles, England became the epicentre that "conjoined [the] birth of capitalism and the modern state system".[1] By 1925 the British Empire spanned almost 25% of the Earth's land area.[2]

To achieve global supremacy, the ancient kingdom had to transition from the feudal model that was embedded in English soil by William the Conqueror in 1066. Under feudalism, all the land was "held of the king". Land assigned to the barons and knights came with strings attached: they drew Rent from their estates on condition that they fulfilled certain public duties (primarily, serving as the military arm of the State).[3] There was no absolute ownership of land – to *own* was to literally *owe*. Obligations had to be fulfilled, or the land would be forfeited back to the Crown.

This arrangement had to be subverted if the nobility was to enjoy the luxury of living off Rent without owing the State.

---

1. Adam Tooze (2018), *Crashed*, London: Allen Lane, p.615.
2. R. Taagepera (1997), "Expansion and Contraction Patterns of Large Polities: Context for Russia", *International Studies Quarterly*, 41(3). https://doi.org/10.1111/0020-8833.00053
3. W. Ullman (1966), *Principles of Government and Politics in the Middle Ages*, 2nd edn., London: Methuen, pp.150-192

The evolutionary discipline of honouring personal responsibility for one's actions had to be reframed and detached from actions relating to the way that the nation's income was distributed. That became the great challenge: how to separate the idea of receiving something for nothing from the obligation to work for one's living. Appropriating Rent as private property subverted the ancient theological principle of the *just price*: the exchange of value-for-equal-value.

By a series of shrewd manoeuvres, the nobility triumphed. One of the landmark events was the law they enacted after the Parliamentarians defeated the Royalists in the civil war of the 17th century. In 1660, Parliament enacted the Abolition Act.

Box 3.1 **Landowners defined the "rule of law"**

The civil war of the mid-17th century culminated in the victory of Parliament over the Crown. The landlords who sat in Parliament not only terminated their feudal dues. They introduced their preferred model of tax-and-tenure into England. The injustice embedded in this transformation was noted by a jurist in the 20th century.

Sir Kenneth Jupp was not just a man of action (he earned the Military Cross for bravery during World War 2), or a practising lawyer (he presided for many years as a judge of the English High Court); he was also a student of moral philosophy. His assessment of the Abolition Act of 1660 was recorded in these terms: "Those holding immediately under the Crown shrugged off their dues, while continuing to oblige those lower down the scale to render dues to them. Thus land (whether in town or country) came to be treated increasingly as de facto the absolute private property of head tenants free from obligation to the Crown".*

Under the new law of the land, what was good for the land-owning nobility and gentry did not apply to the peasants of England. Equal treatment before the law was not a feature of the legal structure on which modern England was constructed.

* Kenneth Jupp (2005), *The Rule of Law*, London: Shepheard-Walwyn, p.94.

Box 3.2 **The Culture of Irresponsibility**

Rent seeking, by corrupting society, undermined nature

Not paying Rent: consuming social and natural services without paying for them ·········· **Domination:** abusing nature (by polluting without paying) to maximise Rent

Wasting human energy: unemployment of people displaced from the commons ·········· **Depletion:** unsustainable erosion of assets accumulated by previous generations

Reckless governance: budget deficits turned into permanent sovereign indebtedness ·········· **Deception:** to avoid accountability, costs shifted to future generations

---

It deleted the military obligations owed to the Crown. In its place, the monarch would receive a fixed payment of £100,000. This would be raised through a new tax on alcohol, and the Excise duty, which was imposed on the general public in place of the Rent from people who held land (Box 3.1).

The land owners who were redesigning England needed the assistance of professionals in the spheres of finance, law and property if they were to capture the power of the state. If they were to co-opt these emerging professions they would necessarily corrupt public life in general. As the fabric of communities was systematically polluted, the natural world suffered the collateral consequences (Box 3.2).

Figure 3.1 **English wages to cost of living (family of five) 1260-1887**

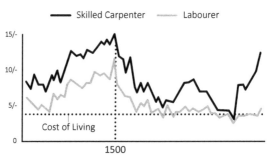

Source: Thorold Rogers, Rev WPD Bliss

The disruptive effects on society were egregiously felt by the peasant and artisan communities. The impact is tracked by the movement of the wages of skilled carpenters and labourers (Fig.3.1).[4] Wages rose from the 13th to the end of the 15th centuries. They then went into an abrupt descent at the beginning of the 16th century, alongside the launch of the land grabs by Henry and the enclosures by the aristocracy. The fall in wages continued for 300 years, with labourers living at or below the bread line.

Free riding and the enclosures

The manipulation of the people of England began when the opportunity to free ride on their backs was enshrined in law and institutionalised through the bureaucracy of the State. This process originated with the misdeeds of a sex-and-money starved king, and the vicious ripple effects were transmitted throughout the globe over the next five centuries.

---

4. The Figure is derived from James E. Thorold Rogers (1890), *Six Centuries of Work and Wages*, abridged by Rev. W.D-P Bliss, New York: Humboldt Publishing.

Figure 3.2 **England's Acts of Enclosure 1500-1914**

Percentage of land enclosed

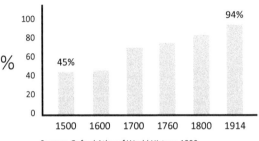

Source: *Oxford Atlas of World History*, 1999

Henry VIII began by demolishing the spiritual life of the nation. This enabled him to grab the monastic lands to pay his bills and fund his military adventures. That was the cue for aristocrats to embark on their mission. The commons of England were systematically enclosed (Figure 3.2). Nor were the lives of other species safe in Henry's reign. In 1532 he enacted the Vermin Acts to legalise the hunting to extinction of creatures like the beaver and lynx.[5]

This was parasitism that threatened the wellbeing of the nation. Why was it allowed to gain a foothold among people who understood what was happening to them? How may the personal preference for the easy life – to live off the labours of others – penetrate society to the point where it undermines the stability of communities?

In pre-urban societies, people were able to censure the would-be free riders by direct intervention. In urban civilisation, free riders have a greater chance of success if they are able to capture the

5. Roger Lovegrove (2007), *Silent Fields: The Long Decline of a Nation's Wildlife*, Oxford: University Press, p. 24.

Figure 3.3 **Hierarchy and the Enforcers of Free Riding**

power of the State. There are multiple hurdles in their way. But if they succeed, a new hierarchy would emerge. This is what happened in England (Fig 3.3).

Henry initiated land appropriation as a formal process by dismantling the monasteries and abbeys. But for that initiative to morph into a fully-fledged process of land privatisation, the feudal aristocrats had to pull off a coup against the monarchy: they had to capture the power of the State. Only then could they control the financial system, to give them the keys to the exchequer. By this means, the landed aristocracy could determine how much revenue would be raised, how it would be raised, and how it would be spent. But the hijack could not end there. For by redirecting the nation's taxable income into their pockets, it would become increasingly difficult to fund the state. So they were obliged to invent new taxes that could be imposed on wages and savings. That, however, did not yield sufficient revenue to balance the state's budget. Their lordships needed a mechanism to fill the deficit. And so, to consolidate their hold over the infrastructure of power, the rent-seekers had to reshape the monetary system. We can trace the way this process evolved with the documents that are lodged at the Public Record Office, which stands besides the Thames in Kew, West London.

The transfer of power began in the 1540s. That was when the commercial market in land was established to facilitate the transaction of the tens of thousands of acres that Henry had grabbed from the monasteries. But his act of sacrilege did not generate sufficient money to assuage his financial profligacy. Beginning in 1545, the currency was debased.[6] This triggered an inflation that caused havoc with the household budgets of the peasant and artisan population, a financial disruption that raged well into the 16th century. While peasants were being driven from their homes, Henry was able to fund his extensive programme of palace building.

Taxation: control of the public purse

In 1450, for the first time, wage earners had been subject to levies on wages of 20s per annum or more. Wealthy people were taxed on land and goods.[7] At the same time, the feudal nobility began to displace peasants to make way for the sheep flocks that returned higher Rents. The ensuing rural poverty was condemned

---

6. W. Shaw (1896), *The History of Currency*, 1252-1896; New York: A.M. Kelley, 1967, cited in Stephen Zarlenga (2005), "Moving Monetary Reform to the 'Front Burner'", *Am Rev of Political Economy*, 3(1), p.63.
7. The statistics, dates and quotations in this section are taken from M. Jurkowski *et al* (1998), *Lay Taxes in England and Wales 1188-1688*, Public Record Office Handbook No 31, Kew: PRO Publications, pp.xli-xliv.

by Thomas More (1478–1535) in his book *Utopia* (1516).[8]

For a commercial market in land, however, we have to turn to the actions of Henry VIII. His initiatives were followed by fiscal innovations that distorted economic activity, one effect of which was to reduce the use of land as the rent-seekers sat back and waited for the capital value of their assets to rise. This enabled them to capitalise on their good fortune.

In 1549, under Edward VI, the loss of productive land required action "in a bid to encourage the cultivation of arable land, which was in decline". The correct strategy would have been to raise the fiscal levies on the land holders, and reduce the burden on capital and consumption. The reverse happened. As a result, distortions arising from the flawed fiscal system were amplified. Policy was framed to "tax sheep-farming and the manufacturing of cloth… the Taxation of sheep and cloth proved contentious and had to be abandoned". As a result, the tax burden was shifted further onto the goods that people consumed, thereby intensifying the regressive character of the fiscal regime.

Taxation took a toll on people's moral sentiments. As the tax-take increased, so did evasion. To survive, cheating had to become part of the way of life. We are told by researchers who peruse the ancient parchments that "Attempts to correct abuses were doomed to failure because evasion was all-pervasive, reaching the highest echelons".

Banking on the financial sector

To cope with budget deficits, the aristocracy had to guide complex forces with overlapping interests which shaped the emerging financial sector.

---

8. Thomas More became Archbishop of Canterbury and was beheaded on 6 July 1535 for offending Henry VIII.

1. *Governance*: the irresponsible nature of the public's revenue system required a flow of credit to cover the annual budget deficits, the loans then being converted into permanent sovereign debt.

2. *Communities*: once they were rendered volatile, tools had to be devised to maintain some semblance of equilibrium. Money lending became one way to profit from the distortions created by taxation.

3. *Individuals*: people are eternally alert to the possibility of profiting from low-risk activities. With the State emerging as its leading customer, the money market attracted funds from investors.

The outcome was a structured evolution of the credit system that was biased in favour of rent seeking. This was not a healthy way to achieve homeostasis, but it enabled some people to prosper. Leading the way were the goldsmiths of London. One of the influential actors in the formative period of 16th century finance was Thomas Gresham (1519–1579), described by his most recent biographer as "arguably the first true wizard of global finance". On behalf of the English Crown, Gresham manipulated the value of sterling on the Amsterdam bourse, creatively designed a variety of ruses to help the state cope with its financial crises (such as forced loans with rigged interest rates, and a scam involving the market for lead), and manipulating the London money market in ways that helped the state to juggle the budget. Gresham did not receive a salary. Instead, he was rewarded with grants of land, the annual income from Rent yielding £400 a year. He laid the foundations of his fortune in 1553 by securing land that had been grabbed from monasteries. [9]

---

9. John Guy (2019), Gresham's Law: *The Life and World of Queen Elizabeth 1's Banker*, London: Profile Books.

Corporations

The market-distorting behaviour of multi-national corporations in the 21st century cannot be understood without tracing their origins through three stages.

1. **First stage:** Piracy laid the foundations for the global adventure that morphed into the appropriation of territories on an epic scale.

Dr Anton Howes, a British historian of innovation, notes that up to 1550, England was Europe's economic and cultural backwater. Other countries were ahead on metrics such as the production of wealth, art and empire building.[10] What stimulated the push that would construct the most extensive empire in history? It was not the vitality of the population: Howes noted that, from the mid-1550s, England suffered severe food shortages, and the threat of famine would be ever-present for the next 150 years. France was the pre-eminent power. England was weak in naval power and revenue collected by government.

During two decades beginning in 1550 there was an explosion of activity. It was all to facilitate one major change in the nation-state: the onset of rent seeking. Squeezing Rent out of other people's territories was the name of the game. This drove the age of sea-faring (charting new routes to resource rich lands) and innovation (in spheres that served the nautical enterprise, such as cartography and ship-building). Notorious characters emerged and were celebrated as national heroes in London's courtly circles. Among them were Francis Drake, a pirate who plundered Spanish galleons, and John Hawkins (he led the way in creating the trans-Atlantic slave trade). Privileged access to the skills that underpinned these nefarious activities was extended to the children of the nobility.

---

10. https://antonhowes.substack.com/

The free riding culture was transmitted to underpin a territorial empire based on slavery and supplanting other people from their land.

2. **Second stage:** the law that enacted joint stock companies enabled people to invest in distant operations without direct participation in the way profits were made.

The nature of this legal entity, from the outset, was based on privileges that empowered the companies to operate with techniques driven not by competition, but by ruthlessness and rootlessness. An early model was the East India Company. It originated with piracy but morphed logically into the role of a surrogate state. Armed with a royal charter, it built an army and took over a sub-continent, which was smoothly inherited by the British state to become the crown jewel in the British Empire: India. Adam Smith provided an outright condemnation of its techniques. The company's methods of operation had effects such as "discouraging cultivation" in Bengal – which impoverished the farmers – and pursuing greedy objectives that caused famine. The company would be more productive, noted Smith, if it did not engage in corruption. But here, I confine myself to noting the observation by Smith that "says it all". In Book 1, Ch 9 (p.108) he notes how the monopoly power of the East India Company enabled it to raise prices to eat into the earnings of wage workers, a power that also "eats up the whole of what should go to the rent of the land". Thanks to its law-sanctioned privileges, the East India Company's "profits" included Rent. The company was the architype of the rent seeking multi-national corporation of the 21st century.

The implications for the indigenous peoples throughout the world, based on the law applied by Britain during its land grabbing episodes, was neatly summarised by an American federal judge.

In discussing the colonisation of North America, he noted that "the British title to American territory...excluded the American Indians from all rights except the right of occupancy". This gave the US Federal government carte blanche, for it inherited "the power of extinguishing this right of occupancy by conquest or purchase".[11]

3. **Third stage:** global conquest as the safety valve for people expelled from their homelands by land grabbers.

The displaced people of the UK had to be found new land on which they could be settled. Thomas Malthus provided the rationalisation for dealing with what was termed the surplus population, on which was blamed the extensive state of poverty. Curating this final stage was Cecil Rhodes, the empire builder who wanted to construct a railway across Africa from Cape Town to Cairo. His fortune was made from diamonds excavated from South Africa. He justified his mission in these terms:

> In order to save the forty million inhabitants of the United Kingdom from a bloody civil war, our colonial statesmen must acquire new lands for settling the surplus population of this country, to provide new markets.[12]

No audit was undertaken of the assault on the lives and cultures of the indigenous peoples who were displaced from their homelands.

Lawyers and the re-constitution of England

The irresponsible nature of the emerging form of governance could not have been embedded in the law of the land without the willing support of the legal profession. Lawyers cooperated with monarchs to shape the narrative that accommodated the way in

---

11. Henry Sumner Maine (1890), *International Law*, London: John Murray, p.74.
12. Letter written by Rhodes in 1895, quoted in William Simpson and Martin Desmond Jones (2000), Europe 1783-1914, p. 237, London: Routledge.

which the subjects of kings and queens were defrauded by land grabs and the rigged fiscal regime. One such person was Nicholas Bacon (1510–1579). He was called to the Bar in 1533. After the dissolution of the monasteries, Henry granted him extensive lands. He loyally served the monarch, and he made clear his desire to emulate the nobility (he was knighted by Elizabeth I). He displayed his aspirations through the homes he built. Redgrave Hall had to be large enough for 20 members of his family and rooms for many more servants. He embarked on the construction of another home in 1563 on the site of "a thousand acres of land and 250 of woods [which] offered a suitable outlook".[13] How many families might have dwelt and earned their living on those 2,000 acres? How many beaver and lynx might have co-existed in those 250 acres of woodland? Historians do not explore such questions.

The devices that created the narratives which shaped the "unwritten constitution" were reviewed by Richard Gordon, a British QC. The legal devices originated with Henry VIII's notion of the "King in Parliament", established in the 1530s and enforced "with savage penalties for those who demurred". After all, notes Gordon, "If those who conquered were to retain power, it was convenient to devise associative ideas that would suggest or reinforce the legitimacy of their authority. This association might be a ritual or a doctrine, or even a symbol".[14]

The divine right of kings resulted in a doctrine that would become of special significance for parliamentary politics. Sir Edward Coke, the Lord Chief Justice of his time (the mid-17th century), presented his theory of parliamentary sovereignty in his *Institutes* (1644). By then, absolute power was consolidated not in the Crown, and not in the people, but in the hands of the landlords who sat in Parliament.

---

13. Alan Simpson (1961), *The Wealth of the Gentry 1540-1660*, Cambridge: University Press, p.55.
14. Richard Gordon (2010), *Repairing British Politics*, Oxford: Hart Publishing, p.12.

Box 3.1 **The land/law nexus**

Alexis de Tocqueville visited America and wrote about its politics in
Democracy in America (the English translation was published in New
York in 1838). He attributed the primary role in the formation of politics
and property rights to land-owning lawyers. He noted the roles of
lawyers like Thomas Jefferson, who had drafted the Declaration of
Independence. De Tocqueville concluded: "The more we reflect upon all
that occurs in the United States, the more we shall find that the lawyers,
as a body, form the most powerful, if not the only, counterpoise to the
democratic element in the Constitution".

  The foundation documents of the US were crafted by plantation
owners (in Jefferson's case, he was also a slave owner), who happened
to be lawyers. In his Reith Lectures, Jonathan Sumption, a former British
Supreme Court Judge, noted that the lawyers of America, as a class, had
acquired the beliefs and influence of the old landed aristocracy. They
shared its habits, its tastes and, above all, they shared its contempt for
popular opinion. There was only one other country that de Tocqueville
could think of where the legal elite enjoyed a comparable influence over
public affairs. That country was Britain.*

* Jonathan Sumption (2019), The Reith Lectures: Law and the Decline of Politics,
Lecture 4.

The legal grip on the land of England was completed with the
fraudulent Statute of Frauds (1677). This required the *holders*
of land to prove that they were the lawful *owners*. The peasants
failed the test, because their traditional rights were not embossed
on parchments. Their rights to the commons were recorded in
tradition. The aristocracy and gentry, however, were shrewd.
When they acquired monastic land, they insisted that their rights
be recorded in legal documents. And so, the proverbial coach
and horses could be driven through the rights of the peasants as
Parliament enacted the enclosure acts that converted the commons
into the private property of the landlords. For their services, the

legal profession was granted the special status that enabled it to capture a slice of the nation's Rents through their fat fees.

A revealing insight into how a constitution could be rigged by lawyers to favour rent seeking was provided by the French author Alexis de Tocqueville (Box 3.1).

Bureaucracy and accountability

One measure of the integrity of a State is the performance of its bureaucrats, the administrators who facilitate the functioning of the power structure. In the formative years of the tax State, civil servants were willing to succumb to the temptations created by the complex web of fiscal policies and political intrigues. Cheating was no longer just an individual failing. It was institutionalised when, in 1563, the assessors engaged in administering the revenue were told that they would no longer be sworn to present true assessments.

William Petty was among those who exploited the opportunity to become rich at other people's expense. By profession a teacher of music, he switched to the role of civil servant when he was invited to map lands that had been confiscated in Ireland. In the process, he enriched himself to the tune of £9,000 – a princely sum in the 17th century – and he appropriated 18,000 acres for himself.[15] Petty was to achieve fame as the compiler of the first national accounts of England. Should we be surprised that, so far as tax policy was concerned, he favoured levies on consumption rather than on Rent?

As the revenue system assumed increasingly arbitrary characteristics, the tax state was forced to find a balance between its revenue needs and the money it could collect. In some places, according to researchers at the Public Records Office, "liable taxpayers took turns paying the tax". The accounting system fell

15. John Guy, *op cit.*, p.224.

into disrepute: by the time of Elizabeth 1, "the lay subsidy had already ceased to be either an effective tax or an accurate gauge of the wealth of the kingdom".

The occasional mass protests by the peasant and artisan populations came to nothing. They laboured under high rates of inflation, and by the 17th century they were ensnared with a Poll Tax levied on their heads. They were unable to transform the course of development ordained by Henry VIII. Police and military power was exercised to protect the interests of the rent-seekers who occupied the political junction boxes that directed the laws of the land.

A clean sweep

The nobility triumphed! They and their hangers-on captured the State that became the largest empire the world had ever known (Box 3.2).

Politics and laws are now administered according to doctrines (such as "equality before the law") that confuse rather than clarify people's rights. Citizens are not equal – when measured in legally sanctioned outcomes – even in countries that are ardent in their commitment to liberty and democracy. In reality, as we shall see in the next two chapters, laws are administered to secure the privileged treatment of one class of property owners. The concept of free rider, while acknowledged in the economic literature, conceals more than it reveals. This is illustrated by the UN's definition:

Free Rider: someone who enjoys the benefits of a (public) good without paying for it. Because it is difficult to preclude anyone from using a pure public good, those who benefit from the good have an incentive to avoid paying for it – that is, to be free riders.[16]

16. Inge Kaul *et al* (eds), *Global Public Goods: International Cooperation in the 21st century* (1999), UN Development Programme; New York: Oxford University Press, p.509.

Box 3.2 **Anatomy of a state capture**

Henry VIII legalised free riding in the 16th century, and the virus of rent seeking mutated through the centuries to pollute and compromise the democracies of the 21st century.

- ▶ **17th century:** intervention of the gentry through civil war; they captured the law-making powers of the State to consolidate their hold on land.
- ▶ **18th century:** Parliament and the constitution were shaped to restructure tax policy. This secured the privileged treatment of Rent.
- ▶ **19th century:** the explosion in productivity through industrialisation was guided to ensure that the net gains were captured by the owners of land.
- ▶ **20th century:** universal suffrage and an authentic democracy were successfully thwarted by disallowing the reintroduction of the Land Tax.
- ▶ **21st century:** corporate technocracy completed the control of the popular discourse by privatising most of the Rents of the radio spectrum (the impact of which is discussed in Book 3).

The UN confines the term to publicly-funded services from which people cannot be excluded (such as the provision of law and order, or military defence). This is a soothing definition: it avoids disturbing people who seek comfort in the argument that the private appropriation of Rent is not immoral. It is, after all, lawful!

Free riders fit into two categories.

1. *Active appropriators* of value by people who do not work to earn it, such as landlords who collect Rent from the users of land. Rent excludes the profit from resources such as dwellings, which are the product of labour.

2. *Passive appropriators* of Rent such as the owner-occupiers of residential property. They are co-opted into this role. When Beatle Paul McCartney bought his Regency townhouse in London for £40,000 in 1965, he did not intend to capitalise on the failure of governments to charge him the full price for the services that accrued at that location. The Rent that accumulated over the subsequent 50 years was capitalised into the selling price of the dwelling. The property was reported to be worth between £10-15m in 2019.[17]

The statistics, crude though they may be, reveal the success of the original land grabs that turned into capture of the British state. In 2016, the Office of National Statistics estimated that urban land was worth £5 trillion. This was 51% of the total net worth of the UK. Figure 3.4 reveals that, in the year 2,000, UK land as a percentage of GDP eclipsed both the rate of growth in the value of dwellings, and the capital that people use to produce tradeable goods and services.

What, in terms of the vitality of the social system, is the significance of this outcome? Consider the macro-economic implications. The income received from the formation of capital (whether as bricks-and-mortar dwellings or combine harvesters that operate on farms) is dwarfed by the gains from owning land and nature's resources. Rational people naturally gravitate towards maximising investments in land and rent-yielding assets, rather than engaging in other forms of activity. That co-opts them into a culture that can only be described as a process of cheating; because the ensuing value is extracted from other people who create it by their labour.

---

17. Emine Sinmaz (2019), "Day clipper...Macca's row over pruning trees at £15m home", *Daily Mail*, August 22.

Figure 3.4 **Non-financial assets as % of GDP (UK)**

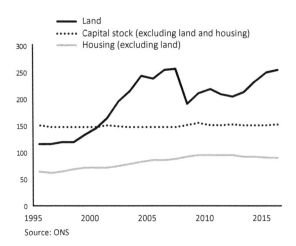

Source: ONS

Thus, the culture of cheating biased the evolution of the British economy in favour of the pursuit of *unearned* income, and against the formation of capital that *adds* value to the wealth of the nation. This bias systematically reshaped behaviour and moral sentiments. People in the 17th century did not need to read a 21st century economic textbook to learn that Rent had been defined as a *transfer income*! From the 18th century, during the emerging Industrial Revolution, the entrepreneurial spirt was compromised by the ever-present temptation to invest resources in land-based assets rather than value-producing activities.

The estimates of the quantum of Rent are substantial. But as we shall see in Ch. 4, they are a grotesque under-statement of the price paid by working people to support those who lived by free riding. Responsibility for that price is not attributed to the formation of the modern state. Instead, the political discourse today emphasises events that followed the Thatcher/Reagan era. Political theorists do acknowledge that "The origins of these nation states were to be found in the association between military power and the ownership of land".[18] But they do not scrutinise the role of rent seeking as the central pillar of the culture which now shapes the destiny of humanity.

18. Bill Jordan (1985), *The State: Authority and Autonomy*, Oxford: Blackwell, p.160.

CHAPTER FOUR

On the Rack:
Taxation and Free Riding

Adam Smith's intervention was perfectly timed: 1776, just as Britain was beginning to transition into a new way to create wealth. Political prejudices needed to be abandoned in favour of a new model of governance, so that people could efficiently employ innovative technologies to elevate the quality of their lives while establishing a new trading relationship with the rest of the world. The model that Smith elaborated in *The Wealth of Nations* identified the principles and practices for operating within a moral framework that would enhance social solidarity. The spiritual sentiments, as these were evolved over time immemorial, would revive to empower people to honour their personal responsibilities to others as well as to their natural habitats.

Members of Parliament proclaimed their admiration for Smith. They honoured him at dinner parties. But they ignored his prescriptions for the construction of a post-feudal society. Instead, they continued with the avaricious habits that had guided the reformation of the English state over the previous 200 years. One measure of the damage that this inflicted on the nation is called the "excess burden" of taxes. This is the loss inflicted in each and every year since the first tax was imposed on people's wages.

By the second decade of the 21st century, the tax regime was depressing productivity by about £500bn a year. Economists will contest my calculation. Alternative estimates would range from a low £150bn (my estimate of what HM Treasury might recognise, based on its flawed modelling), to a sum that was nearly double my central forecast of the annual losses inflicted on the UK.[1] But even the lower estimate reveals a sum that is so large that the people of Britain need not have endured austerity-based political policies that have persisted for centuries. I am content to work with my estimate on the grounds that this offsets the accusations that I am both under- or over-estimating the losses.

The annual shortfall in wealth and welfare is the price paid because Parliaments of both Left and Right persuasions failed to adopt the Smithian formula for funding public services. If the Ground Rent proposal had been adopted as the annual revenue raiser, the UK would be producing a surplus. Under this arrangement, output would be sufficient to fund an Annual Rent Dividend to each person. Instead, the legacy of perverse politics based on rent seeking is a sovereign debt burden that is inflicted on generations as yet unborn.

Our concern in this chapter, however, is not with the conventional assessment of the deadweight losses from bad taxes. These ignore the full human costs. The theoretical models employed by post-classical economists assume away the harsh realities of bad taxes. Their starting point is the delusion that the capitalist economy is grounded in competition. Deviations are branded as anomalies that can be regulated out of the system on a case-by-case basis. This camouflages the Big Lie: competition drives the economy. It was not, in the time of Adam Smith, and is not, now.

From the outset of the Industrial Revolution, Britain embarked on a course of rack-and-ruin. The material achievements cannot

---

1. Fred Harrison (2016), Ch 6 in *Rent Unmasked* (ed: F. Harrison), London: Shepheard Walwyn.

be contested, as measured by the output of consumer products. People live for much longer now than they did then (but the privileged live longer, by as much as 12 years, than others). But carefully camouflaged beneath the headline statistics was the vicious depletion of humanity itself. The loss of human resources cannot be quantified in cash terms. We need to understand what happened, and how it happened, if we are to have any chance of reversing the course on which the free riders embarked in the times of the Tudor and Stuart dynasties. The starting point is the definition of what is meant by rent seeking.

As the techniques of free riding evolved, the appropriation of rent assumed a variety of legal and illegal forms. Some of these were listed by Anne Krueger, a professor of economics, as including bribery, corruption, smuggling and black markets. She interpreted the psychology that underpinned rent seeking in these terms:

> In most cases, people do not perceive themselves to be rent seekers and, generally speaking, individuals and firms do not specialise in rent seeking. Rather, rent seeking is one part of an economic activity, such as distribution or production, and part of the firm's resources are devoted to the activity (including, of course, the hiring of expediters).[2]

The impact measured in cash terms is a small part of the consequences when governance fails in its duty of care to its people. We begin to get a sense of the nasty secret that lurks in the interstices of the rent seeking society when we realise that *the quantum of net income that would surface as Rent and be shared by everyone is diminished*. This is a puzzling statement that was unravelled by Joseph Stiglitz in an article he wrote for a popular magazine. He affirmed that post-classical economists had distanced the market-distorting concept of rent seeking from the classical concept of Rent. But the impact of those distortions

---

2. Anne O. Krueger (1974), "The Political Economy of the Rent seeking Society", *Am Econ Rev*, 64[3], p.293.

did not, in fact, alter the reality. The measurable Rent that could otherwise be shared is reduced by the tortuous wrecking tactics of privilege-seeking entrepreneurs.

Stiglitz repeated that the word "rent" was originally used to describe what someone received without producing anything. This contrasts with "wages," which denotes compensation for the labour that workers provide. But the term "rent" was extended to include monopoly profits.

> In their simplest form, rents are nothing more than re-distributions from one part of society to the rent seekers. Much of the inequality in our economy has been the result of rent seeking, because, to a significant degree, rent seeking re-distributes money from those at the bottom to those at the top. But there is a broader economic consequence: the fight to acquire rents is at best a zero-sum activity. Rent seeking makes nothing grow. Efforts are directed toward getting a larger share of the pie rather than increasing the size of the pie. *But it's worse than that: rent seeking distorts resource allocations and makes the economy weaker. It is a centripetal force: the rewards of rent seeking become so outsize that more and more energy is directed toward it, at the expense of everything else.*[3]

The total pie shrinks as a result of the distortions, which include transfers and subsidies from the government; laws that make the marketplace less competitive; practices that encourage CEOs to take a disproportionate share of corporate revenue…and policies that enable corporations to profit by degrading the environment. By following the money trail, we discover that taxes deplete the quantum of Rent that would otherwise be available to fund the common good. But it gets worse.

---

3. Joseph E. Stiglitz and Linda J. Bilmes (2019), "The 1 Percent's Problem", *Vanity Fair*, May 31, 2012. Emphasis added. https://www.vanityfair.com/news/2012/05/joseph-stiglitz-the-price-on-inequality

Rack-renting humanity

Under competitive conditions, wage earners would be free to exercise the right to reduce their Rent payments to landlords. With Labour and Capital mobile, and Land fixed in supply and location, and if Rent was collected as society's revenue, people would, indeed, be able to negotiate down the level of Rents under certain circumstances. But the free riders rigged property rights to thwart the workings of a competitive economy. Landlords had a trump card up their sleeves. They controlled Parliament. This gave them the power to shape property rights and tax policies. One effect was to deprive the working population of the liberty to renegotiate their Rental payments to sustain productivity and employment.[4] This became the power of rack-renting, a process which authorises the depletion of humanity's legacy assets on a mind-bending scale. The barbarous outcomes result from the application of three techniques.

I. Reducing commercial costs increases Rent

Landlords grew richer from the outset of the Industrial Revolution by defining what counted as a cost of production. This became evident from the way in which entrepreneurs operated the new railway systems. If they were required to pay Rent to government for the right to emit carbon waste into the environment (part of the commons), that would have increased the cost of transporting coal and passengers. The net income would have been reduced: less left to hand over as Rent. So the pricing system was tailored to ensure that the cost of waste disposal was paid by the birds in the skies and (200 years later) the people who were made to suffer from floods and fire caused by shifts in weather patterns.

---

4. One outcome is the upward-only Rent revision clause in leases signed by tenants who want to locate their businesses in commercial properties in Britain's high streets

If, at the outset, the industrialists had to pay Rent for the privilege of dumping waste into the atmosphere, they would have had a financial incentive to use science and technology to contain the carbon emissions within their new technologies. Instead, the pricing system was rigged to favour the maximisation of privatised Rent. This embedded the streak of authorised irresponsibility into the industrial economy.

► In the 19th century: *dumping* carbon into the heavens. Nature's capacity to absorb the waste emitted by the new technologies was treated as a "free" service. By not covering the cost of those emissions, the Rent of coal extracted from the land of the aristocracy was inflated.

► In the 20th century: *dumping* plastic into the oceans. Nature's capacity to absorb the waste that resulted from scientific innovation, such as the by-products from petroleum, was treated as a "free" service. By not covering the cost of this waste, the Rent of petroleum was inflated.

► In the 21st century, *dumping* junk from satellites in near-earth orbit. The European Space Agency estimates that 900,000 pieces of debris larger than 1 cm rotate around earth as hazards to space stations. By not covering the clean-up costs, solar system Rents will be pocketed by future corporations.[5]

The engineers who invented the combustion engine 200 years ago were not aware of the ecological consequences of their actions. But even if they did possess that knowledge, governments would not have adapted their fiscal regimes. The coal seams were buried beneath the estates of the nobility, and they were determined to maximise the resource Rents from fossil fuels.

5. Of almost 4,500 satellites in orbit, only 1,500 were active, according to Johann-Dietrich Wörner, Director General of the European Space Agency (Sarah Knapton [2019], "Defunct satellites threaten human race, space agency chief warns", *Daily Telegraph*, 27 Nov.)

II. Shifting costs through colonial land grabs

Grudgingly or otherwise, people who were displaced from the commons by enclosures, or who were priced out of work by taxes on their wages, would have to be supported by the State. The cost of funding the Poor Laws would have to come out of Rent. So Parliament developed a strategy for minimising that cost on the land owners. They intensified the appropriation of territories on other continents. This was the cost-free way of dumping the "vagabonds" who had been expelled onto the highways and byways of England by the land grabbers. The indigenous peoples of faraway places could be made to pay the price of land enclosures in England and the highland clearances in Scotland. Outcomes included the sacrifice of the living tissue of humanity, to preserve the flow of Rent into the pockets of Britain's land owners.

III. Rack-renting: the case of Ireland

If landlords can displace people onto sub-marginal land; and if those landlords are free to hold families to ransom – insisting on collecting a Rent that cannot be generated out of the land –

Figure 4.1 **Can Family A live on Family B's income?**

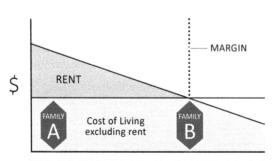

FROM CORE TO MARGIN: RICARDIAN RENT BASED LOCATIONS

something new emerges: rack-rent. This is traced schematically in Fig. 4.1

Family A, which occupies high productivity land, can earn a living while paying Rent. Family B, if it is driven onto low-fertile soil where they can just cover their living costs, can survive only if they are free of the obligation to pay Rent. But if the family is pushed further, on to sub-marginal land, it is faced with a life-or-death problem. It cannot earn enough to cover living costs, let alone produce a net income that could be paid as Rent. That was the fate of many Celtic families in Ireland. If the starving families wanted to survive, they had to leave their homeland. The Celts led the exodus from the British Isles.

Because access to land was not based on the fluid operations of the classical model, many families could not protect their living standards by reducing payments to landlords. All of the negotiating power was in the hands the owners of land. The combination of Rent plus taxes reduced the take-home pay of both rural and urban workers. Their lives were degraded to below subsistence levels. They had one choice only: endure a zombie status, or flee to another country. That is how tens of thousands of people from Ireland ended up in America. The exodus began in the 1680s.

> [A]s competition for the land increased, landlords were able to 'auction off' leases to the highest bidders. That practice, known as 'rack renting,' forced renters to bid more than they could afford to pay. The first great wave of American emigration occurred in 1717-1720 and 1725-1727 when leases granted in the 1690s in the Bann Valley in the west of Ulster expired and rents were sharply increased.[6]

Clergymen achieved notoriety "by bellowing from their pulpits against the Landlords and the Clergy, calling them rackers of Rents and Servers of Tithes...which they know is pleasing to their people". The exodus was via the ports of Londonderry, Belfast and

---

6. H. Tyler Blethen and Curtis W. Wood Jr. (2013), *From Ulster to Carolina*, Raleigh: North Carolina Department of Cultural Resources, p.17.

Newry. Cecil Woodham-Smith captured the tragedy in her book *The Reason Why:*

It was human existence on the lowest scale, only to be paralleled in its isolation and privation, said observers, among the aborigines of Australia and South America. As the population increased, the continual subdivision of farms into patches brought the landlord higher and still higher Rents, and the potato patches of Ireland first equalled what the rich farmlands of England fetched in Rent, and then went higher. Men bid against each other in desperation, and on paper the landlords of Ireland grew rich; but the Rents were not paid—could not be paid. Castlebar was only one of hundreds of estates in Ireland which, prosperous on paper, were sliding into hopeless confusion. "If you ask a man," reported the Devon Commission in 1844, "why he bid so much for his farm, and more than he knew he could pay, his answer is, 'What could I do? Where could I go? I know I cannot pay the Rent; but what could I do? Would you have me go and beg?'"[7]

A Land Commission investigation, in 1830, explained the poverty and distress in terms of the indifference of landlords. "All the landlord looks to is the improvement of his income and the quantity of Rent he can abstract." Once the land is enclosed and deemed to be private property, moral sentiments become infinitely elastic. That was the attitude of the owner of an estate in Co. Mayo.

The Lucan family were one of the major land owners in Castlebar, with an estate of 60,000 acres. The second Earl of Lucan, Richard Bingham, settled at Laleham, on the banks of the Thames in Sunbury, west of London, in 1803. He immediately set about building a new house. He was determined to appoint it with luxury furniture and fine paintings. To achieve this dream, he squeezed his tenants in Co. Mayo. Theirs was a brutal choice: pay the Rent by depleting their psycho-biological condition, or get on a boat in search of land elsewhere.

---

7. Woodham-Smith (1953), *The Reason Why*, London: Penguin, p.104.

Plunder of the legacy assets

The legacy assets of humanity, if they are to remain fit for purpose, need to be constantly renewed. The resources for that renewal come out of Rent. When people are rack-rented, the family as the basic unit of society is ruptured, communities are despoiled, and the moral fabric is degraded. The rack-renting that ruined the Celtic culture was replicated in urban industrial England. In his introduction to the works of Thomas Paine, Howard Fast summarized the impact of life in the 200 years that preceded the Industrial Revolution:

> London of the latter eighteenth century was, for at least half its population, as close an approximation of hell as is possible to create on this earth. [...] The enclosure laws of the previous two centuries had created a huge landless population that gravitated toward the urban centers, mostly toward London, to form a half-human mob, not peasants, not craftsmen – the first tragic beginnings of a real working class.[8]

From this history, we see the human consequences of the discrimination that was written into the law of the land by Parliament in 1660, and embedded into the logic of parliamentary procedure. The tradition of equal access to the use of land, a right evolved by each and every generation from the earliest evolutionary phases of humanity, the one right that made life possible, was brutally cast aside. Nothing changed this status of inequality all the way through to the 21st century: the UN's Universal Declaration of Human Rights, and the European Convention on Human Rights, do not correct that inequality.

► Traditional norms of governance, in which monarchs were viewed as servants of their people (which entitled kings to claim the loyalty of subjects) were reversed.

---

8. Thomas Paine (1797), *Agrarian Justice*, p.ix. https://www.ssa.gov/history/paine4.html

To this day, under the law, people cannot enforce the equal right to the benefits enjoyed by families that consume the nation's Rents.

► Landless people were forced to pay for the right to occupy the land of their birth, hostages to others who had no interest in their welfare.

To this day, millions of able-bodied people endure the humiliation of having to depend on the charitable contributions of others to remain alive.

► Rent – the net income that was traditionally pooled for the benefit of everyone - was degraded so that it no longer served the common good,

To this day, privatised Rent remains the primary tool for discriminating against access to wages, affordable shelter and the good things in life.

To survive as an exclusive class, the earliest rent seekers had to corrupt all of the pillars on which humanity was constructed. This process has steadily evolved over a period of 500 years. At a devastating rate we continue to subtract from, rather than add to, the resilience on which our species relies for its existence. The mortal consequences can be tracked through multiple layers of intervention.

► *Degradation of the economy*: the tax regime drives increasing numbers out of work and into dependency on the State.

► *Deprivation of communities*: social bonds are dissolved, driving people to migrate in search of life elsewhere.

► *Destruction of nature*: co-evolution is replaced by exploitation of Earth and the extinction of other species.

In the natural world, the 2nd Law of Thermodynamics depletes an "energy chain" because "there is less available energy remaining in each successive transformation".[9] Humans evolved because they learnt how to override the systematic depletion of the energy input into themselves and their communities. Their safeguards included the exclusion of free riding, which depletes the flow of energy into the living tissue of which humanity is composed. Today, that energy is drained away, fragmented into a state of disorder – the state of entropy. An unsustainable system has taken control of the equilibrating mechanisms that made possible the evolution of humanity. With the privatisation of Rent, people no longer function within a self-perpetuating system. The rate at which the depletion occurs is determined by the interaction of a dual process.

I The accelerating rate of depletion

The rate at which a society loses its capacity to renew and defend itself is contingent on a at least three processes. These stem from the way in which people are deprived of their share of Rent.

1. Dilution of respect for codes of conduct. If people fail to self-discipline themselves in favour of selfish behaviour that undermines the rights of others, the community begins to dissolve. Stresses include the loss of fraternity. The shift towards a self-centred engagement with others (celebrated as "individualism") may be traced through transformation of morality and spirituality, the codes that were embedded in the human psyche to secure stability within the community.

2. Breakdown of the family as the unit of inter-generational propagation. Through biological and cultural

---

9. H.T. Odum (1995), "Self-organisation and Maximum Power", in Charles A.S. Hall, *Maximum Power*, Boulder, CO: University Press of Colorado, p.321.

reproduction, kinship groups were self-supporting units that transmitted the virtues of empathy and the other sentiments that extended the social relationships. But when the family cannot support itself and becomes a burden on others, the primordial sentiments are replaced with resentment, the loss of dignity and a potpourri of other corrosive emotions.

3. Authority transitions away from a cohesive system of power. Ordinarily, people participate either formally or informally in decision-making processes that affect the common good. Under pressures from rent seeking, the power structure turns into adversarial contests. Coercive instruments are imposed to force people to comply with laws and regulations. This corrodes the social structure and divides the population.

II The rate of co-option into the rent seeking circle

Relationships and the structure of power are altered in response to the accelerated desire to join the privileged circle of free riders.

1. People closest to the inner circles of power are exposed to the privileges enjoyed by rent seekers. Vicariously, they taste the benefits. So they devise strategies for acquiring some of the net income (even if it is only "crumbs off the table"). The flow of Rent has to assuage the appetites of an increasing number of people.

2. Desperate to survive, in time the excluded population learns that "if you can't beat them, join them". People become willing to be co-opted: the alternative is to endure the increasingly harsh consequences of being excluded from the good life.

England was not the first to embark on the course of wholesale destruction of humanity by these means. Spain led the way through colonial appropriation of gold and silver. The port of Seville was the hub of the trade that drew taxes into Spain's coffers (Box 4.1). Archaeologists are to this day stumbling on the destructive impact of Spanish colonialism in the form of abandoned Mayan palaces and monuments.[10]

Plumbing the depths of despair

A consensus is now emerging behind the belief that our world is riven with dangers. My thesis, however, that the primary cause is rent seeking, will be met with objections driven by the fear of one awkward question: how do we redesign the pillars on which our communities rest, to rescue our societies? That question leads to the one remedy that undermines the privileges of free riders. The solution, a change to the way in which people pay for their public services, will continue to be rejected by apologists for the rent seeking *status quo*.

A democratic mandate for change will not emerge until people are convinced about the depth of penetration of free riding behaviour. So we need to subject my thesis to forensic scrutiny. The primary constituents of humanity must be interrogated. If they are found to be depleted, they must be renewed. Has rent seeking left its marks on them to the point where the life-and-death struggle for control over the Social Galaxy is near the point of no return?

If free riding is diminishing the fabric of our authentic being, we should be able to trace the decomposition through three stages. We would be able to measure the rate of penetration of the Social Galaxy's defences (see figure 4.2).

10. Eleanor Hayward (2019), "Discovered in Mexican jungle, lost palace of Mayan kings", *Daily Mail*, Dec. 28.

Figure 4.2 **The Disrupted Social Galaxy**

1. *The zone of depletion*: metrics of well-being are now available to track the rate of decomposition of the biological and psychological health of populations.

2. *The tipping point*: this is the zone where the state of paralysis of power is exposed, to provide a sense of whether we retain the capacity to defend humanity.

3. *The collapse zone*: Has the power of rent seeking driven us to the point where it has overwhelmed the safeguards that were created to protect and sustain human beings? If so, how did this happen?

Box 4.1 **Spain and the "pieces of eight"**

Spain's forays into South America were driven not by intellectual curiosity, or the desire to borrow cultural traits from others. The impulse was the naked desire to ride on the backs of indigenous people who had developed sophisticated civilisations that enabled them to co-exist with rain forests and mountainous regions. To deprive them of their gold and silver, the Iberian conquerors had to crush those civilisations.

Spain's rulers were able to live the good life funded by the precious metals that were shipped to Seville. The "pieces of eight" became a European currency that financed the trade in natural resources that were shipped in from the East. To leverage that economy, tens of thousands of people in America – and slaves imported from Africa – were sacrificed in the fields and in the mines in the Andes.*

For a brief period, Spain became early modern Europe's dominant colonial power. But the resources were squandered. There was no investment in the accumulation of new knowledge. Inflation degraded the value of the products generated by people within Europe. And when the silver ran out, Spain could not fund her mercenary fleets and armies. She slumped into a backwater as others forged ahead in the colonial project.

* Peter Bakewell (1984), *Miners of the Red Mountain: Indian Labor in Potosi, 1545-1650*, Albuquerque: University of New Mexico Press.

To analyse what would become an alien future for society, we need to take account of three features of the propensity to privatise Rent.

► *Control of the rule-making process.* Short of establishing a slave society, the only way to capture a population's net income is by taking control of the state's power. How this was achieved in the UK was discussed in Ch. 3.

► *Changes to the structure of the economy.* The manner in which labour and capital is applied in the production of wealth must be altered. The architecture of the economy is reshaped, with rack-renting as one of the devices.

▶ *Pacifying the population.* A least-cost approach to maximising Rent appropriation was needed. The continuous application of force to intimidate working people to produce Rent would be expensive, and impossible to sustain indefinitely. One solution was to co-opt enough people into becoming free riders so that resistance was viewed as hopeless. This technique is examined in Ch. 6.

The cumulative evidence demonstrates how the moral architecture of society is subverted. Where moral codes had provided security, free riding disrupted the harmony that united populations. Solidarity was replaced by swindling. The resilience of communities was dismantled by the corrosive temptations of avarice. Slowly, at first, incrementally, and then in a pathological stampede, the decencies that guide humans through evolutionary timescales are disrupted by acquisitive greed.

Free riding as a concept has made its appearance in recent studies authored by behavioural psychologists. The term preferred by economists – rent seeking – is noted in their literature, but treated as the deviant acts of individuals rather than analysed as a systemic feature built into the foundations of society. *The values that underpin free riding were allowed to scale up to the point where they overwhelmed people's authentic codes of conduct.*

To achieve their narcissistic goals, it was necessary for free riders to approach their mission ruthlessly. They overwhelmed the planet's eco-systems, to squeeze the maximum Rents out of nature; sponsored military conflicts, to appropriate other people's territories; and inflicted poverty, which was tolerated as the collateral consequence of Rent privatisation.

Rent seeking is now endemic in the globalised community of nations. Responsibility rests with the sovereign nation-state.

Sovereignty was defined in territorial terms in 1648 by the treaties of Westphalia. The relationship between people's spiritual life and the structures of power in Europe was radically altered. The treaties sponsored the secularisation of sovereign power.[11] England achieved this transformation a century earlier, through the interventions of Henry VIII. The arteries of power were corrupted.

1. *Property rights*, which frame the relationship between the exercise of political power and production in the economy, were ruptured in the 16th century. This privatised political and economic power in the hands of a privileged few.

2. *The spiritual life* was integral to the fabric of an orderly life. Henry converted the spiritual domain into a new church over which he presided as the head. This silenced the prophetic voices that might have challenged his behaviour.

3. *Imperial power* became the logical end result of the actions within England, laying the foundations for the globalised economy that could buttress the abuse of power at home.

Tragically, to achieve this outcome, the beneficiaries of free riding had to adopt techniques that would, ultimately, disable the institutions of society, including the structure of power constructed by the rent seekers. At that point, governance would be paralysed. Have we reached that stage?

---

11. Olivier Roy (2019), *Is Europe Christian?* London: Hurst.

CHAPTER FIVE

The Making of
the Culture of Cheating

To hijack the public purse and camouflage their crime, the aristocracy had to supplant what would have evolved into an authentic post-feudal social system with their culture. Their version was anchored in cheating.

Plundering the resources that people pooled for their common good would not have been possible without spilling blood and guts. In England, that happened in the civil war of the mid-17th century. Then, to consolidate their coup, the nobility had to remould morality. Finally, by taking control of Parliament, they would exercise power to manipulate the political destiny of the nation, while shaping the statistics to disguise what they were doing. To unwrap the financial scam, it is necessary to understand how that exercise was executed.

The English aristocracy did capture the state, which gave them *carte blanche* to rack-rent farmers. The looming industrial mode of production, however, presented a threat to their direct appropriation of Rent. Urbanisation would shift more of the production of net income away from farmland and into new locations. A new strategy for milking the population was needed.

Robert Walpole charted the course when, on 3 April 1721, he became the first Prime Minister.

Walpole and the other parliamentarians knew that they were embarked on a perverse mission. John Locke had written a letter to a Member of Parliament, dated 1691, in which he warned that it was futile to tax wages. He published his revelation in *Some Considerations on the Consequences of the Lowering of Interest and the Raising of the Value of Money*. Taxes, he explained, would reduce take-home pay. But people would not be able to live on what was left. So to offset the loss through taxation, they would reduce the Rent that they paid to landlords.

Rent transferred to landlords would be diminished by the amount that the Treasury collected as taxes on earned incomes.

Parliamentarians ignored Locke. They were in the business of denying reality.

Among the early taxes were those on

► windows (1697 to 1851) and on wallpaper (1711 to 1836)

► hair powder (1786 to 1794), and on perfume (1786 to 1800)

► the sale of men's hats (1784 to 1811), and gloves (1785 to 1794)

Anyone caught forging hat-duty stamps could be punished by death.[1]

Such taxes did raise revenue for government, but this also reduced the Rent that would otherwise have been collected by landlords. In other words: *All taxes come out of Rent:* ATCOR!

The nobility and gentry did not think this arrangement was bizarre. Their mission was the restructuring of property rights, along with reductions in the amount directly collected by the Land Tax.

---

1. Ben Schott (2002), *Schott's Original Miscellany*, London: Bloomsbury, p.10.

Manipulating the financial architecture enabled them to weave a web of deceit. False accounting paid off. Walpole was well rewarded: he was elevated as the 1st Earl of Orford. In 1722 he began the construction of Houghton Hall, in Norfolk, funded by the Rent from tenants on the thousand acres surrounding his mansion. He further enriched himself by investing in the slave trade.

One outcome is that we are no longer aware that Rent constitutes approximately half of what the working population labours to produce.

In pre-urban societies, people knew what was happening because they were personally engaged in pooling their net income to fund the common good. In urban society, the scale of living required an intermediary. Agencies of the state were required to collect the Rent that would be invested in public services. So when free riders took control of the state, they were able to camouflage the theft of Rent with the aid of false accounting. That is why, today, economic textbooks claim (without supporting evidence) that Rent is 10% or even a smaller proportion of national income.[2]

To recover a sense of reality, to reveal how net income was made to disappear, we need to retrace our steps back to the analysis by Adam Smith.

ATCOR I: The covert shrinking of Rent

The ATCOR principle is counter-intuitive. If an employer deducts taxes out of an employee's wage packet, the employee paid the tax, right? No. The reality is schematically illustrated in Figure 5.1.

We start with the ideal of a tax-free society. If we assume away the deadweight taxes favoured by rent seekers, income would be

---

2. Paul Krugman, the Distinguished Professor of Economics at the Graduate Center of the City University of New York, says he would "love the idea that land should be a really important part of our stories" but – after reviewing the US national accounts – he decided that the numbers were too trivial to matter. Fred Harrison (2015), *As Evil Does*, London: Geophilos, pp.100-102.

Figure 5.1 **The Shrinking Net Income**

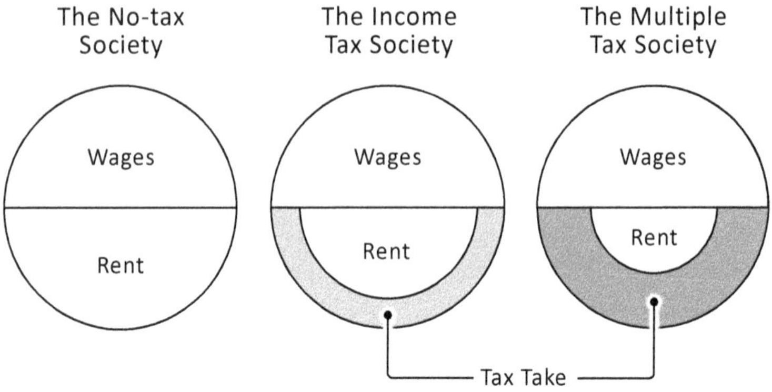

The No-tax Society	The Income Tax Society	The Multiple Tax Society
Wages	Wages	Wages
Rent	Rent	Rent

Tax Take

divided between the value produced by the individual (wages) and the net income which is the result of the cooperative activity of generations past and present (Rent). If people acted according to the principles that had made possible the evolution of humanity, they would devote the net income to funding the services they shared in common.

We then introduce a tax on Wages. The impact reverberates through society and ends up with a smaller sum available as Rent. And so on, as taxes are levied on what people consume (such as the Value Added Tax that was imposed when the UK joined the European Communities in 1973). As the tax-take goes up, the sum that is left as Rent diminishes. ATCOR!

Today, among OECD countries, the average tax-take is around 35% of national income. Rent as measured in the marketplace ranges from 20% to 30% of national income, depending on the point in the business cycle at which it is measured.[3] So the

3. Ronald Banks (1989), *Costing the Earth*, London: Shepheard-Walwyn, pp.40, 177.

long-run average for net income is about 50%. What remains is divided between Labour and Capital as wages and profits.

Once upon a time, people understood what was happening to the value they produced. Even in the 17th century when the Land Tax was introduced, "Although landowners were liable to pay the tax, in many parishes the tenants may have actually paid the tax and claimed the money back from their landlord in the form of a rebate".[4] ATCOR in action. But after 300 years of increasingly complex tax innovations and the wizardry of myth makers, economists now disparage Rent as an inadequate source of government revenue. They claim that Rent is not sufficient to replace existing taxes. They are no longer aware that *taxes are already coming out of Rent!*

So taxes were the indirect way of collecting Rent. But collecting Rent the hard way came at a terrible price, which landlords pushed onto other people.

Over the course of the 18th century, Parliament persisted in its search for ever more creative ways to tax wages so that the revenue collected by the Land Tax could be reduced. This was contrary to the principles of good governance, and despite the intervention of Adam Smith.

Smith went to great lengths to highlight the absurdity of the indirect route to funding public services out of Rent. In *The Wealth of Nations* he provided at least 10 examples of how taxes on wages, consumption and profits were at the expense of Rent. Despite Smith's efforts, one of his admirers, Prime Minister Pitt the Younger, introduced the Income Tax in 1799.[5]

---

4. Mark Pearsall (2011), "The Land Tax 1692-1963", Magazine of the Friends of The National Archives, 22(3). https://nationalarchives.gov.uk/documents/the-land-tax-1692-1963.pdf
5. Today, Parliament continues to promote Pitt's reform as a rational attempt to reform UK taxation. It assures readers that Pitt was influenced by Adam Smith. Pitt, however, wriggled every which way to avoid Smith's proposal for a simple annual Ground Rent. https://www.parliament.uk/about/living-heritage/transformingsociety/private-lives/taxation/overview/incometax/

In the 20ᵗʰ century, ATCOR received thorough analysis by Mason Gaffney, an emeritus professor of economics at the University of California. He provided an exhaustive list of the resources of nature for which people were willing to pay Rent. Those payments might be called taxes, royalties, fees, charges or tolls, but the payments came out of the flow of Rent.[6] Even so, the economics profession continues to stick to the mantra: Rent is a small proportion of GDP.

There are two reasons why the method of raising revenue matters. One concerns the need to hold government accountable. The Ground Rent method is absolutely transparent. Deadweight taxes, on the other hand, undermine the auditing system with the aid of smoke and mirrors. The second reason is that we are all poorer because of deadweight taxes: the economic pie shrinks.

ATCOR II: The shrinking pie

Adam Smith explained how taxes blended a swathe of issues: morality was corrupted, production was diminished and the population was divided into Haves and Have-nots. He registered his outrage in his discussion on the taxes levied on fermented liquor. Parliament justified those taxes on the grounds that liquor tended to "ruin the health and to corrupt the morals of the common people". Curiously, however, those taxes were not imposed on the ale brewed, and spirits distilled, on the private estates of the landlords. They escaped that burden because they were the "rich and great families, where country hospitality is much practised". Smith could not countenance such discrimination. He wrote: "It is difficult to imagine any equitable reason

---

6. Mason Gaffney (1998), An Inventory of Rent-yielding Resources, Appendix 1 in *The Losses of Nations*, London: Othila Press (ed: Fred Harrison). For Gaffney's treatment of ATCOR, see, for example, http://www.masongaffney.org/publications/G2009-Hidden_Taxable_Capacity_of_Land_2009.pdf Gaffney's website is a treasure trove: https://www.masongaffney.org/

why those who either brew or distil for private use, should not be subject to a composition of the same kind".

Indeed, Smith noted, "the exemption, which this superior rank of people at present enjoy, from very heavy taxes which are paid by the poor labourer and artifice, is surely most unjust and unequal, and ought to be taken away". Smith realised that people who regarded themselves as the "superior order of people" would ignore his censure.[7] Not only were the taxes discriminatory; Smith noted that they shrank the total income of the nation.

The gap between actual and potential production grew over time with the advances in science, technology and the increase in the working population (Figure 5.2).

Figure 5.2 **The Indictment Index**

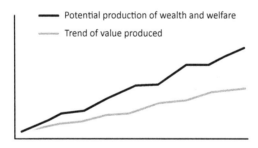

From the onset of the Agricultural Revolution through to the Digital Age, the productive capacity of the British Isles escalated upwards. The first revolution came with the enclosures. It was a brutal affair. An orderly adjustment of tenure was needed, if the opportunities of the looming agricultural revolution were to serve

---

7. *The Wealth of Nations*, Bk 5, Ch 2, Pt 2, Art. 4, pp.419-425.

everyone's benefit. The transition could have been a controlled process as people left the land in the secure knowledge that alternative forms of employment were available in activities such as the cloth making industry. Instead, taxation caused people to work and invest less productively.

We can measure what *could* have been produced, in the absence of taxes on earned incomes. But as we saw in Ch 4, loss measured in terms of the cash value of goods and services does not include the premature deaths that stem from the stresses caused, ultimately, by the erosion of liberty and dignity when people are involuntarily rendered unemployed.

Lost output is an index that indicts governments that privileges the rent seekers and pulverises the lives of the working population. The incremental processes are shown graphically in Figure 5.3.

Recall that Ricardo explained how wages were equalised across the economic space (p.30 above). The line marked AA in the graph is the starting point. It shows that wages across the economy are

Figure 5.3 **ATCOR: All Taxes Come Out of Rent**

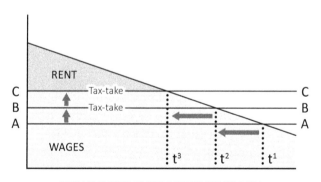

FROM THE CORE TO THE ECONOMY'S MARGIN

approximately equal, and the net income, or Rent, is available to fund the public sector. If an anti-social government imposed a tax on wages, people living farthest from the economic centre would be priced out of work, for two reasons. First, they occupy no-Rent locations. So they cannot shift the tax off their wages, which means they cannot cover their living costs. Second, from an employer's point of view, wage+tax exceeds the work force's productivity. Workers are rendered unemployed. The macro-economic effect is to shrink the economy. The sub-marginal area expands as land is abandoned along with a growing number of displaced people. The margin moves from t^1 to t^2, and then on to t^3.

The rise in the line BB, on the graph, traces the impact on Rent when more taxes are levied. As the economic margin is dragged inwards, the volume of Rent measured in the marketplace decreases. One social tragedy is the crisis of communities that are increasingly marooned in the regions. The problem is not one of low productivity (the explanation touted by politicians to divert attention from them as law-makers). Towns and villages at the economic margin suffer from the tax-driven out-migration of young people in search of employment. Communities are hollowed out, accelerating their depletion into ruin. That is why now, in the 21st century, we hear the plaintive cries for help from regions that have been peripheralised out of the mainstream by the culture of cheating.

Shrinking well-being

Fiscal policies ordained by the landed aristocracy sent ripples through the population, damaging people's health, corrupting the political system and undermining the moral fabric.

Consider the salt tax. People needed salt in their food, which is why it became an early target for taxation. Windows were vital in homes, ensuring the flow of fresh air: so the window tax was introduced, causing many people to brick in the openings. Result: chest and other infections. As for alcohol, it served more than a soporific purpose. Many families drew their water from village streams that were polluted. So they purchased beer which had been brewed, rendering the liquid safe for consumption. Taxes on beer rendered low-income people vulnerable to disease, when they were forced to rely on polluted water for the liquids they needed.

As the tax burden increased and distortions deepened, social pressures arose for compensating subsidies to offset the squeeze on Rent. Subsidies, at first, were genuinely needed to offset the malodorous effects of free riding, which included the monopolies that threatened to drive out competitors. To remain in business, firms appealed to government for special treatment. In time, however, the subsidies became just another route to capture some of the revenue from the public purse – a rent seeking strategy for getting rich without offering commensurate value to consumers.

Parliamentary politics was corrupted. To survive the tax burden, people turned to tax dodging. Again, that device was soon turned to good effect by the rent seekers. To offset the downward pressure on Rent, free riders concocted a doctrine based on what they claimed were the virtues of "small government". Translated, that means: reduce the taxes. What they failed to note was the logical outcome: a reduction in the tax-take automatically increased the Rent collected by those who owned land or Rent-yielding assets.

Through such routes and shenanigans, people were de-skilled and desensitised. The ceiling on the quality of people's lives was artificially lowered, crushing the spirit of the working population. People's welfare was incidental to the overriding objective: what mattered to the new culture of cheating was not how much was collected by government, but how it was collected.

The cumulative effect is that governments are now bankrupt. The UK government, for example, owns "assets of over £2 trillion and liabilities over £4 trillion", according to Richard Hughes.

He once served as Director of Fiscal Policy at HM Treasury.[8] With his insider's knowledge of debt management and Treasury operations, he concluded that the current debt and deficit rules did not allow adequate audit and accountability of policy-makers. So politicians were free to spend the public's money on the basis of rhetoric rather than robust assessments of financial outcomes (Box 5.1).

Box 5.1 **Calculating deadweight**

If the deadweight taxes were replaced with charges on Rent, the four nations of the British Isles would enjoy additional wealth and welfare worth £500 bn a year. This is based on a ratio of 1:1. For every £1 raised by deadweight taxes on earnings and consumption, the distortions to people's behaviour result in a reduction of production by a further £1.

   In response to a Freedom of Information Act request, HM Treasury reluctantly revealed that the ratio of deadweight they used was 0.3:1. This is a trivial ratio which, in 2019, nevertheless translated into a loss of about £150bn! So even if the Treasury can be relied upon to give an honest account of the impact of its revenue-raising policies, the UK lost a sum that far exceeded what ought to have been spent on hiring the additional teachers, nurses and policemen who were needed to deliver efficient public services.

* Fred Harrison (2006), *Wheels of Fortune*, London: IEA, pp. 30, 43-44m 155, 165. Pdf available from https://iea.org.uk/publications/research/wheels-of-fortune

---

The transmission mechanisms

In GDP statistics, no allowance is made for the dissolution of the synergy that integrates people in their communities. There is no measure of the loss of the integrity and vitality that are needed to

---

8. Richard Hughes (2019), Seeking public value: *The case for balance sheet targeting in fiscal policy*, London: Resolution Foundation, p.42.

sustain fellowships, the power that delivers the agreeableness of living in secure relationships. But we can trace the causes back to their origins if we follow the money trail. That trail is not one of statistical correlation but the flow of causation.

By privatising Rent, the malevolent influences are transmitted throughout society. This is schematically illustrated in Figure 5.4. There are three routes to the human tragedies.

1. Direct and immediate impacts of Rent privatisation.
   One consequence was, and remains, the under-funding of public services.

Figure 5.4 **Causation versus Correlation**

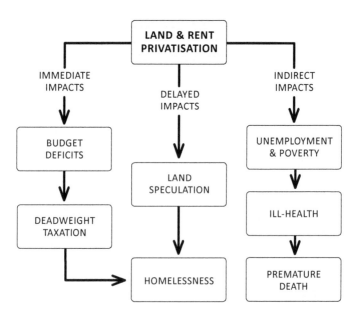

The tax-state's roundabout way of raising revenue, by taxing wages and profits, fails to yield sufficient funds to sustain the services that people need. Government budgets lapse into deficit. Over time, sovereign debts accumulate to the point where they assume a life (better expressed as a tyranny) of their own. New taxes are invented (or tax rates are raised), and under the burden of debt repayments the welfare of working people haemorrhages away.

2. **Delayed impacts** of Rent privatisation. The ripple effects that are transmitted through time. One route, resulting from the privileged treatment of Rent, is through land speculation.

As speculators got richer, the generations that were displaced from their rights to land were forced to resort to alternative ways of surviving. Some of them were forced to migrate to other countries. Others turned to anti-social behaviour (to vent their frustrations) or unlawful activities (to acquire the resources they needed to survive). Through the generations, a segment of the population becomes dis-spirited, and some people lapse into a downward spiral that includes drugs and homelessness. Some demoralised people end up in prison (Box 5.2).

The housing market's impact on wellbeing enables us to trace the cyclical effects of the tax-and-tenure model. The earliest episodes of land privatisation marginalised people who became "vagabonds" (the first Vagabonds Act in England was enacted in 1572). The vagabonds struggled through the generations, constantly colliding with the unaffordable price of land. Today, throughout the rich western world, millions of families cannot afford the price of shelter. Many are rendered homeless: some are forced to sleep rough in the streets, others to dwell in temporary accommodation provided by governments and charities. The scale of suffering is indicated by the data for England. In 2018, an estimated 82,000

Box 5.2 **Suicides in prison**

Suicides in the prisons of England and Wales rose to 91 in 2019. These were preventable deaths according to Sue McAllister, the prisons and probation ombudsman. She attributed the increase to underfunding of the Prison Service, a rising prison population and a lack of staff. The under-funding was due to the austerity policy.* Austerity is attributable to a fiscal regime that represses the productivity of the economy.

The ombudsman also recorded that psychoactive substances continued to be a "significant challenge in prisons" - high security establishments in Britain are easily penetrated by the inward flow of drugs for inmates. Inefficiencies included the outdated procedures for recording the property of prisoners, which added to the costs of running the prisons.

Among the costs arising from the under-funding of the prison system was the additional £100m that the Ministry of Justice was forced to spend to try and close the drug smuggling routes into prisons.

* https://www.ppo.gov.uk/news/ombudsman-disappointed-at-continued-failure-to-implement-agreed-recommendations/

---

families were consigned to temporary accommodation, transients in what is supposed to be their homeland. Their 120,000 children endured ruptures to relationships and schooling, which prejudices their prospects as they enter adulthood.[9]

Children shuttled from one grubby temporary abode to another are the victims of the noblemen of old who triggered the inter-generational deprivation, the painful consequences of which lurk in the shadows of every city in the land. Governments employed a variety of techniques to contain the discontent. These included (in the UK) the Poor Law palliatives that consigned the social outcasts to a state of permanent dependency.

---

9. Wendy Wilson and Cassie Barton (2018), Comparison of homelessness duties in England, Wales, Scotland and Northern Ireland, House of Commons Library, Briefing Paper No 7201.

3. Indirect impacts of Rent privatisation. The impacts that are indirectly transmitted through intermediate events such as unemployment and the ensuing poverty.

Tens of thousands of people every year suffer from premature death, the result of what would otherwise be avoidable ill-health and homelessness. The economics of foreshortened lifespans as a function of the spatial distribution of Rent is well-documented.[10]

One visible effect is urban sprawl, as unaffordable housing obliges people to search for dwellings in cheaper locations. Sprawl generates multiple ripple effects.

► Sprawl forces people to transport themselves in cars, causing the deterioration in air quality. This, in turn, causes respiratory illnesses and death.

► Long distance commuting to work ruptures family life: families are neglected. Opioids may provide relief from stress, but they contribute to premature death.

► Fiscal incentives encourage developers to knock up shoddy dwellings. Jerry-builders were not confined to the Victorian age. They reappeared in Britain in the 21st century.

One major outcome of these effects is a reduction in the overall level of productivity of the economy.[11] The ripple effects came thick and fast in the second half of the 20th century, as populations in Europe's Welfare States demanded remedial action. But the political responses failed to correct the tax-and-tenure system.

---

10. Fred Harrison (2006), *Ricardo's Law*, London: Shepheard-Walwyn, Ch. 8. For one account of the regional outcome of this process in the USA, see Robert Manduca (2019), "How national income inequality in the United States contributes to economic disparities between regions" March 27, Washington, DC: Washington Centre for Equitable Growth. equitablegrowth.org
11. John Muellbauer (2018), "Housing, debt and the economy: A tale of two countries", Oxford University, Discussion Paper 855. economics.ox.ac.uk

Instead, governments intervened with palliative measures that were funded out of deadweight taxes. So the policies either did not work; or, through the ratchet effect, they increased the losses that people endured. These outcomes were the consequence of a society that had become irresponsible.

The Irresponsible Society

Rent seeking is grounded in a doctrine of irresponsibility. This is required, to justify the unwelcome intrusions into people's lives. It also serves to avoid being held accountable for the effects. Irresponsibility manifests itself at all levels of life, including direct impacts on individuals, in the realm of politics and in morality.

I Cheating and the individual

People are not born as equals before the law. Life chances are prejudiced by the codes of conduct that were sanctioned by those who formulated the culture of cheating. The burden of taxation affects individuals in many ways that are not obvious at first sight. One manifestation is the obesity pandemic.

In Western Europe, the UK has the worst record. According to the OECD, obesity has reduced the average life expectancy by nearly three years.[12] The cost as measured by reduced productivity is equivalent to 3.4% of GDP. The cash loss is an average of an extra £409 a year on people's tax bills to fund treatment in the NHS.[13]

OECD countries spend about 8.4% of their healthcare budgets on treatment for overweight-related diseases, including diabetes, cancers and heart disease. But the OECD confines its interrogation of the obesity pandemic in terms of superficial remedies like food

12. https://data.oecd.org/healthrisk/overweight-or-obese-population.htm
13. https://www.dailymail.co.uk/health/article-7557909/Obesity-shaves-THREE-YEARS-average-life-expectancy-Britons-report-finds.html

and menu labelling, the regulation of advertising of unhealthy foods for children, and the advocacy of exercise. The OECD fails to highlight the role of taxation: it creates poverty (which encourages the consumption of cheap, unhealthy foods), and triggers the stresses that drive unhealthy behaviour.

The cumulative effect of the tax burden (including forcing mothers to work who would otherwise choose to devote more time to the welfare of their children), has resulted in over one-third of children being overweight in their final year in primary school.

II Cheating and society

Communities would flourish under the Annual Ground Rent formula. This knowledge is withheld, however, because scholars (among others) offer partial accounts of the tax regime and the way it truncates people's lives. They tailor their statements (for example) to conform to the "small state/low tax" doctrine. The US Congressional Budget Office, for example, acknowledges that taxes cause people to work less.[14] Distinguished academics like Gregory Mankiw, a professor of economics at Harvard – he was an adviser to President George W. Bush – admitted it in a *New York Times* article headed "I Can Afford Higher Taxes. But They'll Make Me Work Less".[15]

What these experts will not publicise is the alternative fiscal strategy that would enhance the resilience of society, which would result if people enjoyed greater control over how to divide their time between work and other pursuits, including civic service in their communities.

14. https://www.cbo.gov/publication/52472
15. https://www.nytimes.com/2010/10/10/business/economy/10view.html

III Cheating and morality

To justify the deadweight taxes, free riders promote the idea that problems can be resolved by adopting a "broad based taxes" approach. They claim that this spreads the tax burden widely, enabling governments to continue with taxes that have behavioural consequences. This is a dissembling argument, which accommodates taxes that tend to corrupt people's morals. The IMF estimates that the least corrupt countries collect 4% of GDP more in revenues than their peers. If all countries were to reduce corruption by a similar extent, global tax revenues could be higher by $1 trillion (1.25% of global GDP). That extra revenue would be available to fund much-needed teachers in schools and nurses in hospitals. Furthermore, "lower corruption would increase economic growth, further boosting revenues".[16]

A hint of the dividend that would accrue if taxes were reduced is provided by Jaromir Benes and Michael Kumhof. They calculated that a cut in distortionary tax rates, by almost 5 percentage points for the labour income tax rate, 4 percentage points for the capital income tax rate, and just over one percentage point for the consumption tax rate, would boost US output by 10%.[17] In 2012, when the authors undertook their study, that would have equated to $1.6 trillion. That is one shocking measure of the losses inflicted by deadweight taxes, but it is dwarfed by the gains that would accrue from the complete removal of those taxes.

16. IMF (2019), *Curbing Corruption*, Washington DC, p.x.
17. Jaromir Benes and Michael Kumhof (2012), The Chicago Plan Revisited (Revised 2013), Washington DC: IMF Working Paper, p.63. The IMF issues a disclaimer: the views expressed by the authors do not necessarily represent the views of the IMF.

The mind-wrenching question

To convert Rent from a benign to a socially malevolent stream of energy, free riders succeeded in converting culture to suit their anti-social behaviour. Politics and the economy were compromised. People's aspirations were corrupted. Some of the distortions surfaced in the labour and capital markets. And so

► *wages*: trade unions fought for monopoly power to raise rates paid to their members above competitive levels, which disadvantaged other workers;

► *profits*: entrepreneurs formed cartels to rig prices above the costs of production, which disadvantaged others from entering the market;

► *rent*: in its privatised form, this became the malevolent mechanism in the capitalist economy, suppressing the quality of people's lives.

Researchers have assembled a great deal of data to reveal the degree of penetration of the problems facing humanity. In the US, Anne Case and Angus Deaton compiled the evidence on mortality in middle age, with causes characterised as "deaths of despair". They link premature deaths to mental and physical ill-health, deteriorating job prospects, social isolation and relationship breakdown.[18] Unfortunately, the dots are not joined up.

Painful questions need to be asked. Is the tax-and-tenure system causally linked to the opioid crisis that is contributing to the premature deaths of large numbers of people in the western world? Opioids contributed to the suicides of 47,600 Americans

---

18. A. Case and A. Deaton (2015), 'Rising morbidity and mortality in midlife among white non-Hispanic Americans in the 21st century', Proceedings of the National Academy of Sciences of the USA (112). https://doi.org/10.1073/pnas.1518393112; and (2017), 'Mortality and morbidity in the 21st century', Brookings Papers on Economic Activity, Spring. https://doi.org/10.1353/eca.2017.0005

Figure 5.5 **Factors contributing to Shit-life Syndrome**

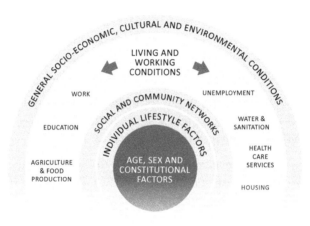

in 2017.[19] Doctors have given a name to the complex conditions that cultivate deep-seated discontent. They call it the "shit-life syndrome", reports Will Hutton, the principal of Hertford College, Oxford.[20] The medical evidence for this syndrome is over-whelming.[21]

The statistics, however, while they reveal symptoms, are not traced to their source. This is illustrated by a review of the medical literature that yielded a rainbow shaped graphic of contributing

19. Centres for Disease Control and Prevention, "Drug Overdose Deaths", https://www.cdc.gov/drugoverdose/data/statedeaths.html
20. Will Hutton (2018), "The bad news is we're dying early in Britain – and it's all down to 'shit-life syndrome'", *The Guardian*, August 19. https://www.theguardian.com/commentisfree/2018/aug/19/bad-news-is-were-dying-earlier-in-britain-down-to-shit-life-syndrome
21. Steven H. Woolf *et al* (2018), "Changes in midlife death rates across racial and ethnic groups in the United States: systematic analysis of vital statistics", *British Medical Journal*. https://doi.org/10.1136/bmj.k3096

factors (Figure 5.5).[22] This is a comprehensive *description* of the penetration of the malign forces at work, but not an *explanation* of the root cause. The statistics encourage piecemeal palliative action of the Good Samaritan kind (laudable). But these studies have an unintended consequence – accommodating, and therefore perpetuating, the cause (or causes) that erupt as epidemics. In essence, what chemists call *valence* is dissolved: communities fall apart.

But if people cannot handle the pressures of life, why blame the tax system?

If free riding *has* captured the power of the state, and if the rent seekers *did* design the accompanying culture to serve their selfish motives, would this damage people's mental health? Were free riders forced to subordinate people's minds to their acquisitive needs? If so, does this mean that we are not in charge of our thoughts and feelings? That we have been co-opted as accomplices to the crime against humanity?

---

22. G. Dahlgren and M. Whitehead (1993), "Tackling inequalities in health: what can we learn from what has been tried?" Working paper prepared for the King's Fund International Seminar on Tackling Inequalities in Health, September 1993, Ditchley Park, Oxfordshire. http://www.euro.who.int/__data/assets/pdf_file/0018/103824/E89384.pdf

CHAPTER SIX

The Psychotic Consciousness

Originally, the human mind-set as it evolved out of nature was shaped by space and by time. These are the variables that physicists interrogate in their search for the laws that guide the universe.[1] Time, and space. For humans, there was a growing consciousness of the time it took for seasons to unfold to shape the resources they needed within their habitats.

Time, and space. The growing seasons, and territory.

Food in the belly from the land, and the time in which to love and live, and to plan the future. Cycles of harmony, working with nature and society. Peace of mind, but an imagination that questioned time, and space, to visualise new ways of living. But all the time, intuitively aware of the limits and opportunities afforded by time, and space.

Evolution from hominin to *Homo sapiens* could only be accomplished by accommodating the spacetime imperatives. Culture was evolved to help the individual to take account of the spacetime realities.[2] The mind-set, one of the legacy assets transmitted through the generations, was framed with reference

1. Carlo Rovelli (2017), *The Order of Time*, London: Allen Lane.
2 Anthony Giddens (1991), *Modernity and Self-identity: Self and Society in the Late Modern Age*, Stanford (CA): Stanford University Press, p.37.

to both the spacetime endowments of each environmental niche, and the accompanying culture. And, as anthropologists have demonstrated, timespace contributed to the shaping of the routines of communities that occupied fixed areas of time and space.[3]

So what happens to people who are violently wrenched from the space they occupy? What happens to their minds when they lose control over the timetable that frames the family lifecycle?

If the violence is the result of the eruption of a volcano, the swamping by a tsunami, or the rupturing of the ground beneath feet through an earthquake, people's lives are turned upside down. If they survive, they can rebuild their lives and communities. They may have to gravitate towards a new location, but the "act of God" does not deprive them of control over the lives that survived.

But when free riding ruptures people from their spacetime routines, lives are scrambled. The theft of communal Rent is an act of violence not only on communities (through enclosure of land), but a direct assault on people's minds. And that violence was routinized, so that the free riders could continue to extract Rent from the working population. So random violence had to be transformed into a routine form of assault on people's minds and bodies, as well as their communities.

This violence was initially aimed at others within the home territory, but it was quickly applied to indigenous peoples in colonised lands. Indigenous peoples were dispossessed of their land, and "Past wounds were not forgotten". Those wounds were the result of what Paul Farmer, a professor of medical anthropology at Harvard Medical School, calls "structural violence".

> The term is apt because such suffering is 'structured' by historically given (and often economically driven) processes and forces that

---

3. Eric Hirsch and Michael O'Hanlon, eds. (1995), *The Anthropology of Landscape: Perspectives on Place and Space*, Oxford: Clarendon Press.

conspire – whether through routine, ritual, or, as is more commonly the case, the hard surfaces of life – to constrain agency.[4]

Farmer's fieldwork with indigenous peoples like the Mayan of South America brought him into close contact with the way in which people had been subjected to centuries of humiliation by invaders who appropriated their land and dignity, in the process eroding their cultures. That process of degradation of personality and community, originating in the appropriation of the commons, remains as much a feature of contemporary Europe as Mexico. But we do not have to travel to the Amazon to observe the way in which the collective consciousness of people has been crushed. It is kicking in pain in territories such as Northern Ireland.

Brain-washing was one of the strategies employed to propagate colonial land-grabbers. This could take several forms. Under the guise of saving their souls, indigenous peoples were forced to abandon their spiritual belief systems. Christian missionaries engaged in this process: "[T]he Church engaged in stripping the colonised peoples of their identity and westernising them".[5] Another device was to inform the indigenous peoples that they were mistaken in thinking that they occupied the territory. The British who grabbed the continent of Australia cooked up a legal theory to reinforce their argument: *terra nullius*. For over two centuries, the aboriginal settlers were confronted with that mind-bending proposition. It was not until a High Court decision in 1992 (known as Mabo) that the concept was overturned.

And so we arrive at the painful realisation that modern societies had to be psychotically impaired through the formation of the culture of cheating.

---

4. Paul Farmer (2005), *Pathologies of Power*, Berkeley: University of California Press, p.40.
5. Olivier Roy (2019), *Is Europe Christian?* London: Hurst, p.24.

Spiritual genocide

Psychosis is defined by psychologists as a brain injury or disease, as perceived in conditions such as schizophrenia and bipolar disorders. I employ the concept as denoting the interference in people's lives in ways that disturb their capacity to appraise reality. Mind-sets are prejudiced against best interests. This is not an individual problem, but a collective state that afflicts the whole population. It is a condition that can be monitored in the workings of the mind, the dislocations to which can be traced back to the malevolent intentions of the earliest free riders.

The mutation of rent seeking into a culture that could dominate the world would not have been possible if the collective consciousness that guides people through life was not first ruptured. By compromising the capacity to realistically appraise the nature of their environments, people were rendered vulnerable. That enabled rent-seekers to co-opt innocent people into accommodating behaviour that subverted their vital interests.

The psychoses are not confined to those that affect children in their early years, such as the deprivation caused by deficient parental nurturing. Adults are subjected to assaults on their minds and emotions to the point where they accept as true some ideas that are false. False beliefs lay the foundations for the state of delusion that permits people to be exploited throughout their lives. Intuitively, they may be aware that something is inhibiting them from achieving their dreams, but they are kept ignorant of the artificial barriers that constrain their liberties. So blame is turned inwards, attributed to the shortcomings of the individual. This state of affairs is nurtured by the values, laws and institutions of the culture that privileges rent seeking.

The outcome is a collective consciousness so traumatised that it is not possible to think straight on issues that are damaging to a population's wellbeing.

The intentional conversion of the rational mind into a psychotic state was a logical strategy for the earliest free riders. Infusing their perverse views and values into other people's minds was the cost effective way of controlling the people who had been detached from the commons. By this means, compliance with the needs of free riders could be sustained on an inter-generational basis.

In Europe, the process began late in the 15th century. That was long enough in the past for the foundation injustices to be expunged from people's memories. Through a turbulent period of 500 years the free riders systematically worked to curb the critical faculties of rational people. Their crime, the appropriation of the commons, was legitimised and institutionalised as the private ownership of land and Rent. With the passage of that amount of time, what originated as perverse behaviour of the rent-seekers, unjust in the eyes of the victims, became accepted as normal. Such a society, therefore, is not aware of its psychotic state. And so we arrive at the unpalatable conclusion: today, people are incapable of evaluating the reality of what is happening to them, despite the evidence which may be staring them in the face. This is the state of delusion into which modern societies have been plunged.

In more recent times, however, the pain of the detachment from traditional rights to land remains acute. Ruptured minds are observed in cases where tribal lands were appropriated by Britain, Spain, Portugal and France in the 18th and 19th centuries, a process that continued, in some territories, into the 20th century. The first settlers were violently severed from their homelands. This separated them from the psycho-social sustenance that defined their status as human beings. Relief was (and continues to be) sought in alcohol and opioids. These forms of escapism have failed to smother the anguish caused by the acute awareness of the original injustices. The crimes are now being adjudicated, in some cases, in courts of law.

In Australia, the first settlers arrived 60,000 years ago. Anthropologist Steven Mithen describes how they adjusted to the new landscapes by using their "profound understanding of ecology. They are expert natural historians with detailed knowledge about the cycles of life and death. Yet they also understand their landscape as continuously created by Ancestral Beings, who have no respect for any laws of ecology. There is no contradiction or confusion in the Aboriginal mind: they simply have two mental representations of their environment, located in different cognitive domains." [6]

When the British arrived and grabbed the land, they also ruptured – in a strong sense, they also appropriated – the minds of the indigenous peoples. One immediate impact was the fracturing of personalities. Ancient communities lost their coherence, some of them disintegrating. And the trauma of dispossession was transmitted inter-generationally up to the present day. The damage is monitored in the spheres of biology, psychology and spirituality.

The spiritual dimension is perhaps the one that Europeans would find most difficult to comprehend. How can a group of people, detached from their traditional commons, endure deprivation of a spiritual kind? The evidence was scrutinised by Australia's High Court. It concluded by placing a cash value on the spiritual loss. In 2019, the Timber Creek native title holders were awarded A$2.5m for the loss of their rights. That sum included A$1.3m for the "spiritual harm" which they continue to endure. The court rejected the Federal Government's argument that the sum was excessive. The majority judgement declared: "The compensation for loss or diminution of traditional attachment to the land or connection to country and for loss of rights to gain spiritual sustenance from

---

6. Steven Mithen (1996), *The Prehistory of the Mind*, London: Thames and Hudson, pp.188-190.

the land is the amount which society would rightly regard as appropriate for the award for the loss".[7]

That claim related to 170 hectares of land. The people whose ancestors occupied that territory were each awarded $15,000 in compensation per hectare, for economic and emotional damages. That settlement is dwarfed by the action initiated by the Noongar people of Western Australia. They have lodged a claim for A$290bn as compensation for the loss of traditional rights to 19.4m hectares. The lead claimant, Naomi Smith, explained that "This is about our cultural and spiritual damage, as all the damage to our land".[8] Another law suit, for A$25bn ($17bn), was lodged in December 2019 for economic and cultural loss endured by the exclusion from territories in Queensland that had been occupied by the Bigambul and Kooma aboriginal peoples.[9]

In Europe, the safety value for some people who were cast off their commons was migration to the New World. The opportunity of reversing the flow to Europe was not available to the displaced Inuit or the Native American Indians. In Canada, the consequences were not confined to the psycho-spiritual realms. One disturbing manifestation of the loss of anchorage in resilient communities is the widespread killings and disappearances of Indigenous women and girls. This process was described as "genocide", and Prime Minister Justin Trudeau confessed: "To the missing and murdered Indigenous women and girls of Canada, to their families and to survivors — we have failed you".[10]

7. www.abc.net.au/news/2019-03-13/native-title-high-court-land-rights-spiritual-connection/10895934
8. www.abc.net.au/news/2019-11-29/$290-billion-wa-native-title-claim-launched/11749206
9. James Smyth (2020), "Aboriginal groups sue states for loss of ancestral lands", *Financial Times*, Jan. 13.
10. https://www.nytimes.com/2019/06/03/world/canada/canada-indigenous-genocide.html

---

Box 6.1 **The thermodynamics of disrupted relations**

Both the free riders and those who laboured without enjoying access to the Rents they produced were condemned to alien forms of being, as they adjusted their primal relationships to the thermodynamics of space and time.

Free riders now viewed space as boundless territories which they may own, and for which they therefore owed no obligations to either nature or society. Time horizons could be transcended, inflated to infinity by creating dynasties that clustered around landed property that could be transmitted through generations (primogeniture). They registered their identities in oil-on-canvas, which were passed down the generations.

Displaced people were detached from the relationships that anchored them in a spatially bounded community. Time horizons were eviscerated: they were condemned to living from hand-to-mouth, which fostered a desperation that degraded sentiments such as empathy for others. They struggled to hang on to memories, deprived of the resources that were needed to recall more than the last two generations.

The cumulative effects included the recalibration of emotional attachments. Rent-seekers looked inwards and manifested behaviour such as narcissism, and psychic comfort was sought from a new doctrine: individualism. Displaced people, suffering feelings of bereavement, gravitated to defensive postures such as viewing others with suspicion (out of fear).

The psychogenic split

Displacement from the birthright to land was traumatic because people were literally ruptured from the spatial and temporal reference points on which *Homo sapiens* relied for the evolution out of nature. Personalities that were attached to ancestral homelands were deranged into a state of alienation. In due course, two distinct forms of cultures emerged based on the altered relationships with space and time (Box 6.1). The ensuing pathological conditions found their expressions in a variety of social forms.

One psychological disorder features swing between states of mania and depression. The mental oscillation entails heightened bouts of happiness and energy before the crash into low points. One cultural equivalent of this psychological disorder is revealed in the economy. People *en masse* engage in activities which, through swings between booms and busts, disrupt the production and distribution of wealth. The population suffers an undulating business cycle in which emotions are amplified as working people (ill-served by their diagnosticians, the economists and law-makers) are deluded about the causes of the underlying state which drives the twists and turns that rupture their incomes. Euphoria in the good times is eclipsed by depths of depression in which millions are rendered unemployed, with many of them losing their homes.

The psychotic condition is illustrated by the detachment from reality in ways that are contrary to one's best personal and social interests. Irrational decisions (such as endorsing political policies that subvert one's interests) demonstrate an incapacity to make rational choices. Law-makers may claim that their policies are "evidence-based", but too often those policies inflicted additional deprivations on people who were supposed to be helped. Such outcomes demonstrate a disorderly consciousness at work. But why attribute the malign influence to the culture of Rent privatisation?

If we are to interrogate relevant evidence, the starting point is agreement on the nature of our society as it now exists. But the quest for consensus reveals the first obstacle to reform. The concept of *capitalism* is assigned a flawed definition by diagnosticians that include academics. Furthermore, we cannot trust the commentators who translate the abstract models into popular language. This obstacle to comprehension is not accidental. It is a logical outcome of the defensive measures taken by the free riders of old.

If this is correct, we need answers to three questions. (1) How is the model of capitalism disconnected from reality? (2) How does this serve the interests of free riders? (3) How would such impairments disempower people by inhibiting them from acting rationally? As our starting point, I need to elucidate life at Ground Zero as I perceive it.

Modernity is a binary composition of two uniquely distinct cultures.

The original culture was based on people working to create the value which supported themselves and their families, and out of which they funded the services they shared with others. Behaviour was disciplined by the obligation to pay for the goods and services which were transacted in the private sector. Value-adding work enabled people to improve their lifestyles and the prospects of their children. This model conforms to the evolutionary record (discussed in Ch. 1), and may therefore be regarded as a representation of normality.

The second culture is an artifice. It is composed of privileges, laws and institutions that serve the needs of people who live by riding on the backs of others. Its elements were designed to extract value created by those who work for their living. Therefore, it must be classified as abnormal, when viewed in terms of the dynamics of evolution as described in Ch. 1. *The emergence of this behaviour in an organised form became anti-evolutionary, because it consumed the flow of energy that was supposed to renew and expand the living tissues of humanity.*

The outcome is a binary world of two antagonistic systems that have been forcibly conjoined. Figure 6.1 schematically illustrates the interface between the two cultures. The linkages exist to secure a one-way flow of the net income that is produced in the value-adding system and consumed by those who conform to the culture of free riding.

The outflow of Rent is channelled through two routes. First, Rent is paid directly to the owners of land, and to the owners

Figure 6.1 **Conjoined opposing cultures**

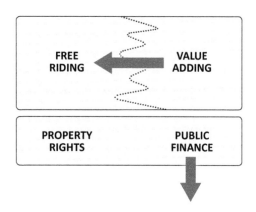

of Rent-yielding assets such as shares in property companies. The second route is the tax system. Part of the taxable value that people produce (which, no matter how we label it, is net income, or Rent) is covertly funnelled to rent seekers. One device takes the form of subsidies to farmers. This value is not retained by the working farmer, but is transferred by tenants to their landowners.[11]

Because free-riding is parasitic, the beneficiaries had to consolidate their privileges in the form of a free-standing culture. This ensured that they could not be dislodged with the ease with which elephants swat blood-sucking flies off their backs.

This binary model is not employed by The Experts to describe capitalism. They ignore free riding as a cultural formation. Some of them do refer to free riding (or rent seeking), but they do not attribute systemic significance to their observations. Consequently, when addressing problems such as unemployment

---

11. An owner-occupying farmer receives two incomes: the wages for his labour, and Rent for the land which he owns. Duncan Pickard (2016), "Enlightenment's Food for Thought", Ch. 10 in *Rent Unmasked* (Ed: Fred Harrison), London: Shepheard-Walwyn

or unaffordable housing, they locate responsibility in the value-adding culture. Disruptions are explained as "market failures", or variants of such *clichés*. Defective features of governance, those that are designed to protect the culture of rent seeking, are ignored.

Three examples illustrate the conceptual failure. One is from academia, the second is from the mainstream media (which interprets and transmits the testimonies of scholars), and the third case is from the community of psychotherapists. The individuals whom I name are not selected because they are extreme examples of the problem. They are typical representatives of an intellectual malaise.

The benchmark model

We begin by recalling the model that was elaborated by Adam Smith (Ch. 2). He formulated the principles for a harmonious relationship between governance, the market economy and the individual. The public and private sectors were conjoined by a disciplined pricing mechanism. This had the effect, in the private sector, of empowering people to undermine attempts at rigging markets with monopoly prices. In the public sector, the norms of economic efficiency and moral probity prescribed Ground Rent as the revenue for funding public goods and services. This integrated model yielded three outcomes.

▶ Post-feudal systems could be constructed on terms that delivered fairness and efficiency on a socially inclusive basis.

▶ Governments that deviated from optimum revenue policies would be exposed by auditing and accountability tools.

▶ Moral sensibilities are nurtured by citizens who, by paying Ground Rent, fulfil their personal responsibilities to society.

THE PSYCHOTIC CONSCIOUSNESS

This is not the model that is taught to students at universities around the world. They are presented with a vulgarised model, which is called capitalism. That version omits rent seeking as a free-standing culture. That culture is the organising mechanism for what is now called globalisation. Because of that omission, the severe stresses that afflict the lives of many millions of people (like unaffordable housing, unemployment and the maldistribution of income) are attributed to the culture that adds value. Anger is directed at the market, and the popular villain is Adam Smith. The devise for directing the guilt onto Smith's shoulders is his single reference in *The Wealth of Nations* to an "invisible hand" (in Bk IV, Ch. 2; p.477 of the Cannan edition).

Branko Milanovic is nominated to represent the academic community. His mission is to instruct us on *The Future of the System that Rules the World*. That is the sub-title of his book, *Capitalism, Alone*. "We are all capitalists now," declares the book written by the Visiting Presidential Professor at City University of New York. As the former Lead Economist in the World Bank's research department, Milanovic is well versed on the global nature of capitalism.

> I define capitalism in the fashion of Karl Marx and Max Weber, as the system where most production is carried out with privately owned means of production, capital hires legally free labor, and coordination is decentralized. In addition, to add Joseph Schumpeter's requirement, most investment decisions are made by private companies or individual entrepreneurs.[12]

In this model, rent seeking is an aberration, not a systemic feature, let alone one that has overwhelmed those who own their labour or the means of production. Adam Smith's "invisible hand" is accorded an appendix, with the interpretation of that concept attributed to recent authors. Milanovic contends that Smith

---

12. Branko Milanovic (2019), *Capitalism, Alone*, Cambridge, MASS: Belknap Press, p.12.

placed his faith in achieving goodness "by relying on individual interests, which in themselves are not always praiseworthy". And, he adds: "The 'magic' that transforms individual vices into social virtues is Smith's invisible hand" (p.227).

Magic plays no part in Smith's model. The arrangements within his model are constructed so that people *automatically* honour their social obligations by paying Rent into the public purse. They do so, *irrespective of their personal attitudes and inclinations, and irrespective of whether they are conscious or not of the implications of their actions.* Three outcomes are routinely delivered with every transaction, as producers and consumers go about their private business. Simultaneously, they

1. *determine the value* of the services provided by both nature and society, specific to each location that is occupied or each service that is consumed;

2. *facilitate the pricing mechanism* that co-ordinates interactions between the public and private sectors, which optimises the allocation of resources; and

3. *honour personal obligations* to defray the full cost of the benefits which they receive, without depriving others of their equal share of nature and society.

If these outcomes are obstructed by constraints imposed by rent-seekers, blame cannot be attributed to "the market" *per se.* Culpability lies wholly with governance for failing to enforce the financial arrangements that would deliver ideal outcomes in practical ways.

Whether intentionally or not, academics like Milanovic distract people from focusing remedial action on the source of their problems: the parasitic culture of free riding. Milanovic, by emphasising selfishness in individuals, reinforces the myths and animosity directed at the "invisible hand".

Academicians deploy mathematical techniques to assess economic problems. This is supposed to enhance the rigour of their reflections. It merely accords spurious statistical precision to what may be ideological prejudices. This is the "magic" that does serve to bias public policies, thanks also, in part, to the interventions of commentators. They inform the mass audiences that elect politicians. The scholastic material in peer-reviewed journals is digested and channelled with the aid of headlines in the mainstream media. One of those commentators is Stig Abell, the Editor of the *Times Literary Supplement* (which he thinks "is the most important publication in the world").[13]

Abell selected himself for our scrutiny by writing an instructional book on *How Britain* Really *Works*. He emphasised the "Really" in his title, by implying that he enjoyed access to knowledge that was beyond the reach of others. So how does he assess our binary world for his readers and listeners? The British economy, he declares, "has been a fantastic success story". That verdict has to be squared with this account:

> We have, in this United Kingdom, an economy that will produce no real wage-growth for more than a decade, has millions working but in poverty, a health service buckling under increased demand, an ever expanding prison population, an unequal education system that fails working-class white boys, a justice system that over-prosecutes black people.[14]

How do we account for this perplexing state of affairs? Once again, readers are invited to focus on Adam Smith's "invisible hand". Abell explains that "The principle behind the expansion of the economy was one of selfishness of each person striving to make money for their families and – in doing so – growing the economy for all". This insight is traced back to Smith, with no

13. Stig Abell's cv includes stints as the managing editor of Britain's biggest newspaper (the *Sun*), hosting talk shows on commercial radio, presenting a radio programme on the BBC and commentating on commercial TV.
14. Stig Abell (2019), *How Britain* Really *Works*, London: John Murray, p.6.

reference to the balancing instrument, the Ground Rent-based financing of the public sector that Smith advocated.

If Adam Smith's model had been instituted, the UK, as the first industrialised nation in the world, would have avoided the involuntary poverty and underfunded public services about which Abell laments. Crime there would have been, and therefore the need for prisons; but not of the kind driven by desperation of working people who were driven off the commons and on to the highways.[15]

The notion of a mono-cultural market economy is false, but it accommodates Marxist doctrines. It also serves the purposes of seemingly shrewd intellectuals like Joseph Schumpeter (1883-1950), who influences academics like Milanovic. Schumpeter's concept of "creative destruction" rationalises the wrecking episodes in the capitalist economy.[16] He presented acts of destruction as an innovative mechanism that eliminated obsolete practices and technologies with substitutes that yielded higher gains in productivity. Recessions were cathartic, conclude his acolytes, for they cleaned out zombie enterprises.[17] This schema helps to distract analysts – and the public – from the wanton waste provoked by a malevolence that lurks unseen within the system.

My third case is taken from the profession of psychology.

Douglas LaBier, a Washington DC-based psychologist, subscribes to the idea of social psychosis. He defines this condition as a "constellation of shared delusions". The detachment from reality had germinated beyond the pathology of individuals, and had contaminated society at large. He deconstructed that

---

15. The land enclosures continue to this day, now taking forms such as the unaffordable prices that deprive people of secure shelter.
16. Joseph Schumpeter (1942), *Capitalism, Socialism, and Democracy*, New York: Harper. This is the third most cited book in the social sciences published before 1950, behind Marx's Capital and Adam Smith's *The Wealth of Nations*.
17. Joseph Schumpeter (1934), "Depressions", in *Economics of the Recovery Program*, ed. D. Brown *et al.*, New York: McGraw-Hill, p.16

collective psychosis into four themes: science and facts; personal values; political and economic ideology; and public and social policy. He was optimistic, however, in believing that the psychotic nature of society was being addressed. His prognosis rested on faith in the individual, and public endorsements for behaviour that promoted the common good.

> By the 'common good,' I'm referring to a broad evolution beyond values and actions that serve narrow, self-interests; and towards those guided by inclusiveness – supporting well-being, economic success, security, human rights and stewardship of resources for the benefit of all, rather than just for some.[18]

These values and expressions of social solidarity are, indeed, part of the popular discourse. Unfortunately, the action needed to convert the fine words into healing strategies is blocked by the defensive postures that protect the privatisation of Rent. Among the obstacles are the psychoses that afflict the health of nations. LaBier does acknowledge the influence of the vulgar version of Adam Smith's model.

> That ideology has also prevailed in our views of adult psychological health and maturity. In essence, this ideology makes the pursuit of greed, self-centeredness and materialism the holy trinity of public and private conduct. And it's generating a growing 'social psychosis.'[19]

That doctrine is the core of the ideology that serves the vital interests of rent seeking, which is why the sweet talk of the "common good" must fail to override the toxic culture of free riding. For evidence of this conclusion, recall the medley of international conferences on the need to combat – for "the common good" – the threats from climate change. Assemblies of the world's governments began in Rio in 1992, continued annually

---

18. https://www.psychologytoday.com/hk/blog/the-new-resilience/201010/growing-social-psychosis-clashes-serving-the-common-good
19. https://www.psychologytoday.com/gb/blog/the-new-resilience/201010/growing-social-psychosis-clashes-serving-the-common-good

through to Madrid in 2019. They were distinguished by fine words and the failure to mobilise meaningful action to allocate resources to curb carbon emissions.

By demonising Adam Smith, we end up with the rewiring of the collective consciousness. This created the space for free riders to continuously propagate as virtuous their versions of property rights and tax policies.

That is the big picture. We now need to drill down to the detail.

Detachment from reality

Douglas LaBier's "constellation of shared delusions" provides a framework for marshalling evidence to test whether modern societies are anchored in a culture that is psychotic. My obligation is to reveal whether that condition is calibrated to serve rent seeking as a socially organised form of behaviour.

Science and facts

Has science been compromised to serve the interests of rent seeking?

Charlatans do misuse science, but we are concerned with those whose interventions damaged the collective mind-set while advancing the privileges of free riders. Herbert Spencer (1820-1903) is our archetype of a social scientist (he is credited with being a co-founder of sociology – the science of society). He abused the scientific method to serve the interests of the landlord class.[20]

While working as a journalist for *The Economist* in London, Spencer wrote *Social Statics* (1851). In this, he excoriated the enclosure of land. Land should be converted into state ownership and Rent diverted into the public purse. Then, Spencer became a regular weekend guest at the mansions of the landlord class.

20. Fred Harrison (2015), *As Evil Does*, London: Geophilos, pp.28-31.

And he expunged his testimony about the evils of private land ownership from the public record.

More was to follow. Spencer read Charles Darwin's theory of natural selection, and he converted biology into a class ideology. He achieved this with a trope: *"survival of the fittest"*. This spin laid the foundations for "social Darwinism".

The effect was profound. It rationalised the culture of class conflict. Those at the top were the fittest, a station in life that was legitimised by biological science. Rather than interpreting the theory of adaptation by natural selection as an evolutionary process based on co-evolution, Spencer originated the notion that war was necessary for the purpose of European state formation. That theory was picked up and propagated by others.[21] Spencer's intervention – by helping to sustain a false collective consciousness – facilitated the emergence of eugenics as a discipline that served Hitler's perverse political ideology.

Herbert Spencer became an honoured visitor in the drawing rooms of the stately homes that were built with the Rents sucked out of the villages of England.

Personal values

Have human sentiments been mangled to accommodate free riding?

The crime began when monarchs and their aristocracies abused their populations by enclosing the commons and privatising the Rents. Today, however, from the point of view of political relevance, the major block of land owners are those described by the right-wing media as "hard working middle-class home-owners"! People are indoctrinated from an early age to *"Get on the property ladder."* The advice is always framed in terms of "owning your own home". Never do the media pundits say: *this is the*

---

21. Francis Fukuyama (2011), *The Origin of Political Order*, London: Profile Books, pp. 27, 487 n.27.

way to rip off the working population by accumulating capital gains from land.

The beneficiaries of the rent seeking culture do everything within their power to encourage their offspring to become free riders while admonishing cheats on the sports field and condemning billionaires who move their assets off-shore to avoid taxes. The roots of perverse actions have been well camouflaged.

Political and economic ideology

Are politicians guided by ideologies that undermine the interests of their constituents?

On the whole, democratically elected politicians are sincere in wanting to help the people who voted them into power. And yet, they routinely enact laws that ill-serve their constituents while enriching the rent-seekers. This outcome arises because they employ palliative measures rather than policies that root out the causes of problems in their communities. An example is the way in which the housing crisis is addressed. The shortfall in affordable shelter has existed throughout the century of universal suffrage. Solutions include tax incentives and cash subsidies which, far from adjusting the price of shelter to what people can afford, serve to raise the cost of dwellings even higher.

Are politicians innocent dupes? There is a problem with that kind of excuse on their behalf. One damaging piece of evidence relates to the lack of transparency in the administration of democratic governments. As the deadweight costs mount, politicians fail to provide a full audit of the damage caused by their tax policies. Instead, they seek refuge behind ideological slogans.

► *Politicians on the Right* campaign for lower taxes by arguing that rich people would otherwise move their assets to other jurisdictions. But they are silent on the fact that *tax cuts are translated into higher Rents, and governments have to reduce what they spend on public services.*

▶ *Politicians on the Left* campaign for higher taxes to fund services, but they do not audit the way in which their taxes inflict losses on the working population. Deadweight taxes reduce employment opportunities and they degrade the quality of the lives of the people whom they claim to represent.

Public and social policy

Are governments complicit in sanctioning policies that undermine people's interests?

Governments proclaim their desire to enhance the health of their citizens. An example is the fine resolution contained in the National Planning Policy Framework presented to the UK's Parliament in 2019. This asserted on page 5 that the objective was

> to support strong, vibrant and healthy communities, by ensuring that a sufficient number and range of homes can be provided to meet the needs of present and future generations; and by fostering a well-designed and safe built environment, with accessible services and open spaces that reflect current and future needs and support communities' health, social and cultural well-being.

Instead, the programmes of governments of both Left and Right ideologies militate against the well-being of their populations. Within the UK, "postcode lotteries" are administered by governments in which outcomes can seriously damage the health of residents. Spatial inequality surfaces in the statistics on physical and mental ill-health. The symptoms are recorded in abundance. They include neuropsychiatric conditions (depression, mental ill-health). And in the UK alone, air pollution is linked to the premature deaths of 40,000 people a year. An estimated

9,000 Londoners die prematurely because of polluted air, partly by inhaling plastic from the tyres of motor vehicles. The closer one's home to busy highways, the greater the risk and the shorter one's life. The disadvantages are inflicted on babies even before birth. The London-based Mental Health Foundation summarises the medical evidence:

> Disadvantage starts before birth and accumulates throughout life... We know that certain population subgroups are at higher risk of mental health problems because of greater exposure to vulnerability to unfavourable social, economic and environmental circumstances, which intersect with factors including gender, ethnicity and disability.[22]

In England and Wales, over 205,000 children were identified as having mental health problems in 2017/18. This was an increase of more than 50% in four years, according to the Local Government Association. Cllr Antoinette Bramble, Chair of the LGA's Children and Young People Board, warned: "We are facing a children's mental health crisis, and councils are struggling to provide the support young people so desperately need".[23] A study of evidence from cities across the UK and Poland by researchers at Kings's College, London, revealed that children living within 50 metres of a major highway were exposed to heightened risk of lung cancer, and the development of their lungs was stunted. Dr Rob Hughes, senior fellow at the Clean Air Fund, said: "Air pollution makes us, and especially our children, sick from cradle to the grave, but is often invisible".[24]

Public policy, far from saving those children, is putting them at risk. Even as the problem grows, the public services that are supposed to help them are being curtailed because of a shortfall of funding of over £3bn.

22. Mental Health Foundation (2016), *Fundamental Facts About Mental Health* 2016, London, p.8.
23. https://www.local.gov.uk/about/news/councils-seeing-more-560-child-mental-health-cases-every-day
24. https://www.kcl.ac.uk/sspp/departments/geography/research/Research-Domains/Environmental-Dynamics/newsevents/newsrecords/air-pollution

This tragic state of affairs will continue indefinitely, if we continue to tolerate practises that perpetuate the delusions that distort beliefs about the prevailing values, laws and institutions. We need to employ the proverbial scalpel to remove the virus within the financial system, if we wish to avoid what is otherwise inevitable: a catastrophe on an existential scale.

My prediction will not be regarded as reliable by people who presume to understand how the world *really* works. People like Stig Abell, who insists that "fortune-telling is a mug's game played by demagogues, charlatans and economists". The primary reason why commentators and their favoured experts cannot offer reliable forecasts is that they are working with asymmetric information.

This is how Wikipedia defines that concept:

> In contract theory and economics, information asymmetry deals with the study of decisions in transactions where one party has more or better information than the other. This asymmetry creates an imbalance of power in transactions, which can sometimes cause the transactions to go awry, a kind of market failure in the worst case.

Asymmetry was built into our minds. The free riders have the advantage of possessing the information that makes them rich, and the rest poor. But that problem is nothing to do with "a kind of market failure". It has everything to do with the failure of governance. And we cannot *see* what is going on, because the rent-seekers managed to capture our minds.

CHAPTER SEVEN

Anatomy of the failed State

History was being made, and I was there. For 10 years I commuted from London to Moscow and St Petersburg to participate in one of the most dramatic social experiments of the 20th century. The fall of communism bequeathed a sacred gift: the chance to nurture into existence a society that complied with the principles which made possible the evolution of humanity.

► *In the East:* China under Deng Xiaoping abandoned communism's command economy and opened the nation to market economics. What would "socialism with Chinese characteristics" look like?

► *In the West:* the Soviet Union abandoned communism under Mikhail Gorbachev. Could Russia nurture a "level playing field" in the marketplace so that everyone might enjoy higher living standards?

► *In the Global South:* South Africa terminated apartheid and Nelson Mandela presided over the crafting of a new constitution. Could colonial racism be erased and people united in the rainbow nation?

Three systemic restructurings: but would they be able to resist the temptations of free riding?

Starting in the 1970s, I argued that, over the course of 400 years, rent seekers had manipulated minds to the point where people were hosts to the alien virus that was eating away at the heart of humanity. Would these three countries prove me wrong?

I was under no illusions as I boarded my first Aeroflot flight. Western governments were determined to persuade countries in Eastern Europe to adopt the capitalist version of market economics. If they succeeded, people who had endured gulags and bureaucratic gangsterism would become victims of the culture of cheating. They needed a reprieve. What they did not need was the "shock therapy" prescribed by Dr Jeffrey Sachs, the Harvard professor who, according to the *New York Times*, was "probably the most important economist in the world".[29] Sachs was an advocate of post-classical economics. He embarked on his mission by promoting the vulgar form of market theories. But western intellectuals did not harbour self-doubts. Western liberalism represented "the end of history".[30] I was determined to challenge that proposition. There *was* a better way to order the affairs of the democracies, and Russia could lead the way. The 1990s would be the testbed for two models: rent seeking capitalism and the competing social Rent model.

We can now look back at the three social transformations to interrogate my claim that free riding had mutated to the point where it was unstoppable. Could it have been otherwise?

Counterfactual narratives must be located in reality. Otherwise, they are fairy stories. Realistically, could the architects of the new systems deliver inclusive justice if they had adopted the Rent-based pathway to social evolution?

29. Peter Passell (1993), "Dr. Jeffrey Sachs, Shock Therapist", *New York Times*, June 27, Section 6, p. 21 of the National edition. https://www.nytimes.com/1993/06/27/magazine/dr-jeffrey-sachs-shock-therapist.html
30. Francis Fukuyama (1992), *The End of History and the Last Man*, New York: Free Press.

The three countries were ideal testing grounds, given their contrasting geographies and cultures. As for the realism of my counterfactual hypothesis, this is affirmed by the presence in each of the three countries of circumstances that favoured the restoration of the social status of Rent.

▶ *South Africa:* with two exceptions, local governments already applied a land tax: this arrangement could be extended under the post-apartheid constitution.

▶ *Russia:* land and nature's resources were in public ownership. Retaining that arrangement and collecting Rent instead of taxing wages was an option.

▶ *China:* land was retained in public ownership and leased to those who needed it. The government could collect Rent instead of taxing entrepreneurial profits.

Conditions were fertile for the application of the classical model of good governance.

It was not to be. Why?

The resurrection of Russia?

An attempt to reform taxation in pre-revolutionary Russia was made by Count Leo Tolstoy, the author of *War and Peace*. He applied his literary skills to promote the economics of Henry George in his novel *Resurrection*. He broadcast his views in the London *Times* and, given his noble status, he even had direct access to Czar Nicholas.

As a land owner, Tolstoy was close to the peasants. He had detected the discontent in rural life. His moral sentiments were aroused, but his initiatives were to no avail.[31] Lenin moved in and

---

31. David Redfearn (1992), *Tolstoy: Principles for a New World Order*, London: Shepheard-Walwyn.

launched a Marxist revolution. Eight decades would pass before the idea of fiscal reform could re-emerge in Moscow, this time from a scholar with enormous influence among the law-makers.

When Mikhail Gorbachev created the space that allowed Boris Yeltsin to seize power, the Academician-Secretary of the Economics Department of the Russian Academy of Sciences was Dr Dmitry Lvov. With the end of the USSR, Lvov had no doubts about the strategic course on which Russia should embark. At all levels of government, including the federal Duma, he advocated the need to retain public ownership of the nation's land and natural resources, along with the liberation of the economy. Governance should be based on revenue from the nation's rich flow of Rent. That, he believed, would result in rapid rehabilitation of society, while fitting the economy to take its place in the global markets.

Lvov tested his theoretical work at the Central Economic Mathematical Institute in Moscow. He not only realised that the retention of Rent was the key to renewing the economy; he also understood that this would deliver "the spiritual and moral renaissance of the nation".[32]

I had read Tolstoy's prophetic works, and I shared his faith in the prospects for Russia. I linked up with Lvov. Our mission was to explain the benefits of a three-pronged programme of reforms.

► People must honour their responsibility to pay Rent for the benefits they received from nature's rich endowments as well as the services from society.

► The economy must to be diversified by privatising the capital assets, to empower the latent entrepreneurism while freeing people from deadweight taxes.

32. Quoted in B.H. Yerznkyan (2016), "Russian Innovation Institutions Development through the Prism of Lvov's Reform Strategy", *Economics & Economy* (4). http://www.economicsandeconomy.me/sites/economicsandeconomy.me/ files/017-27_yerznkyan_s.pdf

► Government was obliged to facilitate the change on
terms that safeguarded people's welfare, by blocking any
attempt to incubate the virus of rent seeking.

I assembled scientists, property professionals and lawyers to
explain that this was a practical project (Box 7.1).

Box 7.1 **Advocates of a moral market**

A global network of altruists travelled to Russia and, for 10 years,
as volunteers, provided Russia with a clear vision of what could be
achieved.

All of the Rent-generating assets were in the public domain, and
could safely remain there while providing access through leases in
return for Rent. This case for reform resonated with the public and
their civil institutions. Retaining urban land and resource Rents in the
public domain, while privatising the right to produce goods and services
without being taxed on earned incomes, would create a moral market.

The team included property professionals from the US (Ted Gwartney
and Edward Dodson), Denmark (Jørn Jensen) and South Africa (Peter
Meakin); professors of economics from the US (Nicolaus Tideman,
Mason Gaffney, Kris Feder and Michael Hudson); a constitutional lawyer
who served as a judge of the English High Court (Sir Kenneth Jupp); a
British farmer/landowner (Dr Duncan Pickard); a town planner from
Australia (Dr Philip Day); and a UK financier (Ronald Banks).

Our goal was a social market that was consistent with the spiritual aspirations of the people. Our initiatives included

► seminars and consultations within the Federal Duma,
and addressing civil society organisations such as the
Union of Russian Cities (which endorsed our proposals);
and private meetings with policy-makers, including
Viktor Chernomyrdin (Prime Minister, 1992-1998);

▶ pilot studies to demonstrate the feasibility of the programme. The study of Nizhny Novgorod demonstrated that, starting with the absence of a commercial land market, a register of location values could be compiled and revenue raised from Rent to fund public services;

▶ publication of studies in co-operation with a St Petersburg research institute, to elaborate on the fiscal formula that could combine the market economy with an inclusive form of governance that would free the population from class divisions and exploitation.

In 2001, I reviewed the record. We had failed. What followed was described by a historian at the Higher School of Economics in Moscow.

Under Putin, the first decade of the 21ˢᵗ century was a time when the state returned in all its former glory: the elite enjoyed their privileges while elections were repressed; the law and the ordinary citizen were regarded with disdain; there was the rhetoric of a great state along with wars for an imperial heritage...This is a chronicle of the state's attack on the individual, the assertion of its sovereign rights on our territory, our body and our memory.[29]

Our speeches, pamphlets and interviews had come to nothing. All the resolutions passed by civil society institutions were ignored. Instead of the Single Tax model as conceived by the Physiocrats and Adam Smith, Boris Yeltsin yielded to the diplomats and university professors from London and Washington DC. State enterprises were privatised on the cheap under the guise of sharing the wealth with the population. "Shares" in the enterprises were sold to sharks who became the oligarchs. Moscow became a victim of what was then called The Washington Consensus. The free riders triumphed.

29. Sergei Medvedev (2019), *The Return of the Russian Leviathan*, Cambridge: Polity Press, p.ix.

Dmitry Lvov's hopes were dashed. The tragedy unfolded before our eyes in streets like Nevsky Prospect, the Oxford Street of St Petersburg.

In the early days, before commercial stores were opened, tradesmen sold their wares out of kiosks located around the high footfall metro stations. Municipal governments licensed the locations for modest sums of roubles. A significant part of location Rent was left with kiosk operators. And so, out of the woodwork emerged the mafia gangs. They offered the tradesmen "protection". The offers came with menaces. The price of the protection equated to the location Rent (minus what was paid to the licensing authority).[30] That model evolved into a state-sponsored version, with "a law enforcement officer offering 'protection' in return for a share in your business".[31]

The "shock therapy" promoted by Jeffrey Sachs had the predictable effect. By 2016, the share of national income received by the bottom 50% had fallen from 30% in 1989 to less than 20%. The share of the top 1% soared from around 25% to over 45% of national income. The price for adopting western property rights and tax policies was registered in this verdict: "[I]nequality levels are comparable, and somewhat higher, than those observed during the tsarist period".[32]

All the pain of the communist experiment, which included the killing of millions of kulaks, had been for nothing.

The West was warned. In 1999, testifying to a US Congressional committee, former CIA operative Richard L. Palmer explained that members of the KGB were among those who were looting Russia's coffers. "We have little time left to avoid the

---

30. Fred Harrison (2008), *The Silver Bullet*, London: the IU, pp.15-16.
31. Maxim Trudolyubov (2018), *The Tragedy of Property: Private Life, Ownership and the Russian State*, Cambridge: Polity Press, p.205.
32. Filip Novokmet, Thomas Piketty, and Gabriel Zucman (2017) "From Soviets to Oligarchs: Inequality and Property in Russia 1905–2016," WID.world Working Paper Series (No. 2017/9).

permanent denigration of the term 'democracy' in this region and the return of totalitarian regimes which may not necessarily be Communist." [33]

The USA gained from the brain drain. One thousand mathematicians gave up on their motherland. They migrated to the US, where they contributed massively to productivity even as Russia's productivity was locked into a downward spiral.[34]

Within Russia, the shock therapy contributed to the collapse of life expectancy among middle-aged professional men in the 1990s. By 2005, 37% of Russian men died before the age of 55, compared to 7% in the UK.[35]

Ayuka Tserenov was a witness to the state of dejection. Under Vladimir Putin's presidency, fiscal mismanagement saw the population slump deep into personal debt. Tserenov was a typical case. He took out a mortgage to buy an apartment which he could not afford. He then had to take out further loans to service the mortgage and to cover living costs. In 2019, in his province of Kalmykia, people had slumped deep into debt. Tserenov testifies: "I have seen fathers and sons stop talking because of loans, couples get divorced – some people even killed themselves".[36]

Dmitry Lvov summarised the political failures of the transition years. Writing in 2001, he noted that Russia was losing $15bn annually to corruption; organised crime controlled about 40% of private firms and 60% of public enterprises, and the share of banks under the control of the mafia was around 85%.[37]

33. https://archives-financialservices.house.gov/banking/92199pal.shtml
34. George J. Borjas and Kirk B. Doran (2012), The Collapse of the Soviet Union and the Productivity of American Mathematicians, Cambridge, MA: National Bureau of Economic Research Working Paper 17800 http://www.nber.org/papers/w17800
35. David Zaridze et al (2014), "Alcohol and mortality in Russia: prospective observational study of 151 000 adults". https://www.thelancet.com/journals/lancet/article/PIIS0140-6736%2813%2962247-3/fulltext
36. Max Seddon (2019), "Russians feel weight of debt burden", Financial Times, Aug 30.
37. Lvov, D. (2001), "Rent as Public Revenue: The Strategy for Russia's Breakthrough to the Future", Geophilos, No. 01(1). http://www.cooperative-individualism.org/lvov-dmitry_rent-as-public-revenue-2001-spring.pdf

Russia did have a political choice. Her politicians were provided with the evidence of how to reconstruct their nation on principles of economic efficiency and moral integrity. They abandoned the people in favour of a kleptocracy that was enriched out of the nation's Rents.

Middle course from the Middle Kingdom

For 2,000 years, stasis prevailed. Except for the innovations introduced by the Song dynasty (960-1279 AD), China remained a slumbering giant waiting to be plucked. That humiliation occurred in the mid-19th century, when the anchors of gunboats from Britain, France and Germany were dropped off her coast. Historians offer generous explanations (such as the commitment to the values of Confucius) to explain The Great Slumber, but the primary reason was the wasteful use of the nation's net income (Box 7.2).

By the second half of the 19th century, however, China could have embarked on a new course. We begin our assessment with the fiscal policies of the Qing dynasty, which began in 1644 and was terminated in 1911.

In the 18th century, 70% of government revenue was derived from a land tax.[38] Political power, however, remained centralised, and the spirit of enterprise was absent. Knowledge of how to put state revenue to better use began to percolate in from the West, primarily through Sun Yat-sen (1844-1925). He had studied medicine in Hawaii, and travelled in the US and the UK where he read the works of John Stuart Mill and Henry George. His manifesto – *Sun Min Chu I* (Three Principles of the People) – charted a new course for the nation: modernisation would emerge

---

38. Debin Ma (2011), "Rock, Scissors, Paper: the Problem of Incentives and Information in Traditional Chinese State and the Origin of Great Divergence", Department of Economic History London School of Economics Working Papers No. 152/11, p.26. http://eprints.lse.ac.uk/37569/1

Box 7.2 **China: cultural stasis**

Nathaniel Peffer researched the reasons for the collapse of Chinese civi-lisation. He noted that the high level of educational achievement did not benefit the people. "The urban masses as well as the peasantry lived on a bare subsistence level, and not too securely on that level." The ruling dynasties did not nurture the working population. "Injustice, cruelty and indifference to the welfare of the masses were accepted as the natural state."*

But what happened to the Rent that peasants generated on their farms? Why wasn't this invested in the dynamic evolution of Chinese society? Yi-Fu Tuan, the distinguished Chinese American geographer, explained how "many small landlords...were content to live off their rents and enjoy their leisure rather than work and invest their income in enlarging their holdings".†

The net income was dissipated. Tucked safely away on the eastern edge of the Eurasian landmass, the rent-seekers could slumber as they sapped the creative energy of the peasants. That state of affairs prevailed until Europe's traders turned up and insisted on selling opium to the nation's drug addicts in exchange for the resources that could be transported back to Europe.

* N. Peffer (1931), *China: The Collapse of a Civilization*, London: George Routledge, pp.16, 26.
† Yi-Fu Tuan (1977), *Pace and Place*, London: Edward Arnold, p.57.

---

through the investment of the nation's Rent in a revitalised social infrastructure.[39] It was not to be. Dr Sun led the revolution that displaced the dynasty in 1911.

Mao Zedong (1893-1976) opposed Dr Sun's approach to reform. He had read the works of Karl Marx. Battles raged for 30 years, until Marxism prevailed. By the late 1970s, however, the Politburo came to realise that the Marxist model was not working.

---

39. Fred Harrison (2012), *The Traumatised Society*, London: Shepheard Walwyn, p.120ff.

A new programme was promoted as "Socialism with Chinese characteristics". Were the reforms guided by the egalitarian values that are supposed to underpin the socialist doctrine? The answers, again, are located in the treatment of the nation's net income.

Land and nature's resources did remain as the collective property of the people. Use rights, however, were privatised.[40] This was appropriate, if leaseholders were required to pay the Rent of their holdings into the public purse. The way in which this could be achieved was highlighted in speeches delivered in China by a German professor of taxation at Trier University of Applied Sciences. Dirk Löhr, who is also a tax consultant for a Heidelberg law firm, organised seminars to which contributions were made by Rent-as-public-revenue advocates that included a lawyer (Terry Dwyer from Sydney), property professionals (Bryan Kavanagh from Melbourne and Ted Gwartney from Los Angeles), and myself. The Politburo in Beijing was left in no doubt about the fiscal model that would deliver a social market economy.

The guardians of the nation's property failed. Rent was privatised. This opened the door to rabid forms of free riding in both the private and public sectors.

In the private sector, entrepreneurs and salary workers engaged energetically in property speculation. They assembled portfolios of apartments not so much to lease out as to hoard for the capital gains. Thomas Piketty and his colleagues assessed the outcome. Private wealth rose from around 100% of national income in 1978 to over 450% of national income in 2014, largely due to the privatization of residential property. China reached a level close to those seen in France, the US and the UK.[41] The gap between the

---

40. Zhenhuan Yuan (2004), "Land use rights in China", *Cornell Real Estate Review* (3).
41. Thomas Piketty, Li Yang, and Gabriel Zucman (2017), "Capital Accumulation, Private Property and Rising Inequality in China, 1978–2015," WID.world Working Paper Series. https://wid.world/document/t-piketty-l-yang-and-g-zucman-capital-accumulation-private-property-and-inequality-in-china-1978-2015-2016/

top 10% of income earners widened from the bottom 50%, whose share of national income declined.[42]

The optics appeared in the form of ghost towns: vast numbers of new skyscraper blocks standing empty, a testimony to the waste of capital. According to researchers at South-western University of Finance and Economics in Chengdu, vacant units amounted to more than one-fifth of China's entire urban housing stock.[43] Land speculation and its associated waste of capital became as much a rent seeking preoccupation in China as in the UK and USA.

In the public sector, the culture of cheating appeared in the form of extensive corruption of civil servants by property developers. In 2014, as part of his anti-corruption campaign, President Xi Jinping ordered the National Audit Office to investigate government land sales. Reuters reported that this was likely to "disclose the rent seeking and corruption phenomenon in various areas" linked to the property sector.[44]

Western observers, operating with their blinkered analytical models, were deluded. They cheered China for driving down global poverty rates. According to the World Bank, poverty (measured as people existing at or below $1.90 a day) had declined dramatically: 800m had risen out of poverty, most of them Chinese citizens. The *New York Times* reported that "The American Dream is Alive. In China".[45] But China's accomplishments were assessed in terms of the authorised model of economic growth as taught in western universities. That is why western economists began to study China for lessons that might be learnt. But there was no magic quasi-socialist formula driving China's growth rates. People had simply been freed to work and fulfil some of their aspirations. Missing

18. https://wir2018.wid.world/part-3.html
43. Linda Poon (2019), "China's Huge Number of Vacant Apartments Are Causing a Problem".citylab.com
44. https://www.reuters.com/article/us-china-corruption-land-idUSKBN0GG04020140816
45. Javier C. Hernandez and Quoctrung Bui (2018), "The American Dream is Alive. In China", *New York Times*, November 18. nytimes.com

from the inquests was the issue of what *might* have been achieved, if the model championed by Sun Yat-sen had been adopted after World War 2, when Chairman Mao finally triumphed.

According to Dr Sun's model, if Deng's China had retained Rent in public ownership, while untaxing earned incomes, the social transformation would have been even more remarkable than the double-digit growth rates that were achieved in the economy. That counter-factual claim can be tested with empirical evidence.

We can compare the record of Communist China with the performance of the people who settled on the island of Formosa. Their story began with the defeat of the government that had remained faithful to Dr Sun's doctrines. The red army fought a running battle against Dr Sun and his successors until Mao won. In 1949, Dr Sun's Kuomintang Party sought refuge on the island they renamed Taiwan. The Kuomintang laid the foundations for a new social system that was grounded in the philosophy bequeathed by Dr Sun. Land owners were pensioned off in a Land to the Tiller programme. A land tax was instituted.

The first Asian Tiger was born.

Table 7.1. **One Culture, two Systems**
Taiwan and Communist China

GDP per capita: $ (PPP)			
	1950	1973	2018
Taiwan	922	3,669	52,304
China	614	1,186	18,200

What might have happened on mainland China if, instead of a communist victory, the Kuomintang had been allowed to implement Dr Sun's doctrine? Mao's economic record can be compared to what unfolded on Taiwan. Table 7.1 tracks the progress of the two economies. The divergence in GDP cannot be explained in terms of differences of psychology or cultural history: both populations came from a common biological stock and shared a cultural past. The difference was due to Dr Sun's Three Principles of the People doctrine. The Taiwanese thrived while their mainland cousins died by the million in the attempt to embed in their minds the lessons in Mao's Little Red Book.

Mao was so blinded by the diktats in the Marxist texts that he also ignored the achievements of Hong Kong. The British colony was constructed on land leased from China; therefore, the land could not be sold as freehold. The merchants who located on the island were obliged to pay Rent into the British colony's coffers. Outcome: low taxation and explosive growth.

The reasons for the achievements of Hong Kong and Taiwan were ignored after the capitulation of Marxist ideology in 1979. The culture of cheating was free to embed itself in China. The legal preservation of land as public property was not sufficient to inoculate the nation from the virus of free riding. The rent-seekers understood this. Many strategies were available for real estate developers to pluck the nation's Rent. One was to align properties-for-sale alongside schools branded with the names of elite British institutions such as Wellington College and Dulwich College. This attracted purchasers who understood that the net gains from close proximity to good schools could be capitalised into the location Rents of the dwellings.[29] Thus were the people of China co-opted into the culture of free riding.

---

29. Tom Hancock (2019), "UK elite schools gain top marks in China", *Financial Times*, December 27.

South Africa: fiscal apartheid

What would happen if a country abandoned the Rent-as-public-revenue policy? According to our Rent thesis, there would be a measurable deterioration in the fabric of society. This proposition can be tested in post-apartheid South Africa.

Land taxation had been introduced to southern Africa in 1813, in the form of perpetual quitrent tenures. Affordable land attracted European settlers. In 1914, General Jan Smuts proposed to introduce an income tax alongside a land tax. The land tax was opposed. The ATCOR effect made its appearance.

> [N]ot only do income taxes burden GDP and growth, but [...] replacing land taxes with income taxes causes land prices to rise. This unconscionable transfer of wealth to landowners by the State's choice of its tax policy renders unused land unaffordable, thereby preventing unemployed citizens from growing, rearing and building things for themselves.[30]

What happened thereafter was a vicious programme based exclusively on the culture of rent seeking.

► *Land grabs:* indigenous people were dispossessed of their rights. Britain created concentration camps to stamp the new way of life on the territory.[31]

► *Racial segregation:* black people were herded onto "homelands", the marginalised areas located far from white towns and fertile farm land.

► *Gold and diamonds:* the resource rents enriched Britain and Europe, with none of the benefits recycled back to the people displaced from their tribal lands.

---

30. Nicolaus Tideman and Peter Meakin (2016), "Land tax versus income tax: *A historical assessment of success and failure in South Africa"*, in *Income Tax in South Africa: The First Hundred Years* (Editors: J. Hattingh et al), Cape Town: Juta.
31. Fred Harrison (2010), *The Predator Culture*, London: Shepheard-Walwyn, pp.72-74.

The post-apartheid era began with Nelson Mandela. He symbolised the fortitude of the human spirit. His 18-year imprisonment on Robben Island was spent crushing stones. He was invited to negotiate a peaceful transition to democracy. Unlike Sun Yat-sen, however, he did not have a coherent programme of reform. Would universal suffrage deliver an authentic democracy? Mandela was elected president in 1994 and awarded the Nobel Peace Prize. A new constitution was crafted which declared that "We, the people of South Africa…Believe that South Africa belongs to all who live in it, united in our diversity".

Two decades later, I witnessed what this meant as I drove around the shanty towns outside Cape Town. The country that Mandela and his African National Congress (ANC) inherited continues to display all of the characteristics of the free riding colonial culture.

► Previously, towns that were dominated by whites, apart from Port Elizabeth and Cape Town, had taxed land values to raise revenue. This was cancelled in 2004. The standard property tax on both land and buildings was introduced.[32]

► Income distribution deteriorated. The top 1% income share had halved between 1914 and 1993, falling from 20% to 10%. From the end of apartheid, the trend went into reverse, along with a decline in the average national income (Figures 7.1)

► The state was captured by the rent seekers who plundered the public purse. Corruption emerged as a political

---

32. Nicolaus Tideman and Peter Meakin (2016), "Land tax versus income tax: A historical assessment of success and failure in South Africa ", in *Income Tax in South Africa: The First Hundred Years*, (Editors: J. Hattingh, J. Roeleveld and C. West, Cape Town: Juta.

process, prominently featuring President Jacob Zuma.[33]
The state's infrastructure deteriorated, with periodical
power blackouts.

Interracial inequality had fallen throughout the 1980s and
1990s, but inequality within racial groups increased. Today,
according to the IMF, South Africa has the worst record for
inequality in the world.[34] During the election of 2019, people
declared that they were puzzled. They had the vote, which they
were told would emancipate them, but they did not recognise
themselves as enjoying freedom. Some even informed reporters
that they were better off under the previous apartheid regime.[35]

Figure 7.1 **South Africa: Income of the Top 1%**

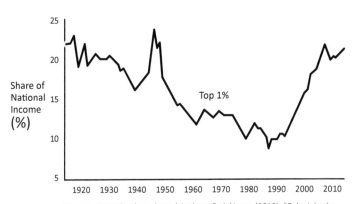

Sources: Facundo Alvaredo and Anthony B. Atkinson (2010), "Colonial rule,
apartheid and natural resources: Top incomes in South Africa, 1903–2007"
(Centre for Economic Policy Research Discussion Paper,) and updates in WID.
World. https://wir2018.wid.world/part-2.html

33. https://www.theguardian.com/world/2019/oct/11/zuma-to-stand-trial-corruption-
charges-arms-deal-south-african-president
34. https://blogs.imf.org/2019/11/07/the-threat-of-inequality-of-opportunity/?utm_
medium=email&utm_source=govdelivery
35. https://www.nytimes.com/2017/10/24/business/south-africa-economy-apartheid.
html

Could it have been otherwise? The fiscal infrastructure was in place so that the transition to a full Annual Ground Rent system for raising government revenue would have presented no administrative challenges. Employment and income prospects would have been raised for everyone. That would have been in accordance with the Constitution. Shanty towns would become obsolete relics of the apartheid era.

South Africa's politicians, and the government Treasury, would have none of it.

A commission was launched to review tax policy (the Katz Commission). It reported that "The mining industry in particular is opposed to the implementation of a land tax because it could act as a barrier to entry to new land owners, its revenue raising potential is relatively low due to high collection costs, redistribution through a land tax system has been proved unsuccessful and its high administrative demands" (p.13).[29] A false appraisal, but that was to be expected from the leading rent seeking industry.

The Treasury, however, could not claim ignorance. In January 2019 it admitted that "The Constitution requires that the taxing power not be used in economically destructive ways. Income taxes and value-added taxes create large deadweight losses by reducing entrepreneurial activity and the incentive to work. These harmful taxes should gradually be replaced with a land-use tax, which are not harmful as they do not distort economic activity". Correct, and the Treasury acknowledged: "Land is an immobile form of capital, which can increase in value due to public expenditures to improve nearby infrastructure". But, pathetically, it added: "National Treasury has been holding and attending workshops to explore this topic". And then, dutifully, it added the get-out clause that rests on wilful blindness: "The instrument can potentially improve the efficiency of the tax system, but is unlikely

29. http://www.treasury.gov.za/publications/other/katz/3.pdf

to be a sufficient source of revenue to substitute all other tax instruments".[30] By closing their minds to the ATCOR effect – all taxes come out of Rent (see Ch 5, p.82) – the guardians of tax orthodoxy excluded the one policy which they admit had all the virtues of fiscal prudence.

From 1996, the foundations for economic policy were laid and presided over by Trevor Manuel, a left-wing firebrand who is acknowledge as one of the leading campaigners against apartheid. This is one verdict on his stewardship:

> His earlier sarcastic comments about the 'amorphous markets' were quickly forgotten; and Manuel soon adopted the economic imperatives of the Washington Consensus...During his long tenure as Minister of Finance he became the darling of South Africa's business and financial community...At the same time, however, he also saw a steady increase in the wealth gap between rich and poor.[31]

Mandela had vowed to render all citizens equal. The Constitution formally pronounced that equality, and claimed that South Africa "belongs to all who live in it". In reality, South Africa belonged to those who extracted the Rents from the richly endowed soil. Mandela failed, but not without first consulting the best brains available. One of them was Ian Goldin, who explains on his speakers' agency website that, as a South Africa native, he had served as chief executive of the Development Bank of Southern Africa and had advised President Nelson Mandela. He went on to serve as vice president of the World Bank before his appointment as Professor of Globalization at the University of Oxford. He is promoted as "One of the world's leading authorities on globalization and economic development".

---

30. South Africa National Treasury (2019), Final Response Document on Rates and Monetary Amounts and Amendment of Revenue Laws Bill, 2018, pp.5-6.
http://www.treasury.gov.za/legislation/acts/2018/Response%20Document%20on%20the%202018%20Rates%20Bill-17%20January%202019.pdf
31. Stephen Meintjes and Michael Jacques (2015), Our Land, Our Rent, Our Jobs, London: Shepheard-Walwyn, p.10.

He was honoured in Davos as a Global Leader of Tomorrow by the World Economic Forum. At a conference on the Greek island of Rhodes, I had the opportunity to ask him whether, with the benefit of hindsight, he would have offered diferent advice to Nelson Mandela. He paused for a moment's reflection and replied: "No".[32]

The self-devouring state

A break with the past in Russia, China and South Africa could only deliver a happier outcome if their net incomes had been invested on everyone's behalf. This was not to be. But they were not alone in suffering from a defective development model. In post-Soviet Hungary, anguished socialist Prime Minister Ferenc Gyurcsany revealed how "I almost perished because I had to pretend for 18 months that we were governing. Instead, we lied morning, noon and night".[33] In Ukraine, the IMF's loan-for-land-sales pushed Volodymyr Zelensky, elected President in 2019, into selling farmland: distressed farmers feared that foreign speculators would deprive them of their livelihoods.[34]

The price is still being paid for the failures of governance. In South Africa, under pressure from the left-behind black citizens in the shanty towns, the ANC government announced that it may have to nationalise and redistribute white-owned land without compensation.[35]

Ominous lessons emerge from our three case studies. Russia, China and South Africa are canaries in the mine. They provide advance warning of the mortal prospects if we allow free riding to capture nation-states.

---

32. DOC Research Institute, 15th Anniversary Forum, Rhodes, 6 October, 2017.
33. www.news.bbc.co.uk/1/hi/world/europe/5359546.stm Excerpts translated by BBC World Service.
34. Roman Olearchyk (2020), "Ukraine sows seeds of suspicion with land sale plans", *Financial Times*, Jan. 20.
35. https://www.thenation.com/article/south-africa-elections-land-expropriation/

► Russia is building her military capability and interfering in the democratic practises of western nations. President Vladimir Putin believes liberalism is no longer viable, and he wants the West to accept his version of a multi-polar world.[36]

► China is employing genocide to tame a million Uyghurs. Genocide was defined by Raphael Lemkin (1900-1959) to include extermination of language, religion and culture. The UN deleted *cultural genocide* from its Convention on Genocide.[37]

► South Africa demonstrates that, unless we integrate people by sharing Rent, fascist attitudes will re-emerge with tragic implications. Anti-Semitism has become an issue in the West. It was a live issue in the UK's election in 2019.

One portrait of our corrupted globalised world was offered by the IMF:

No country is immune to corruption. The abuse of public office for private gain erodes people's trust in government and institutions, makes public policies less effective and fair, and siphons taxpayers' money away from schools, roads, and hospitals. While the wasted money is important, the cost is about much more. Corruption corrodes the government's ability to help grow the economy in a way that benefits all citizens.

But the IMF, while claiming to employ "comprehensive diagnostics on the quality of fiscal institutions, including public investment management, revenue administration, and fiscal transparency", fails to anchor its financial advice in the one fiscal

---

36. https://www.ft.com/content/2880c762-98c2-11e9-8cfb-30c211dcd229
37. Fred Harrison (2012), *The Traumatised Society*, London: Shepheard-Walwyn, pp.vii-x.

strategy that could discipline those who exercise political power over the public purse.[38]

This is the crazy world which we now inhabit, as one psychotherapist put it in language that cannot be turned into fiscal legislation:

> It's obvious that were it not for our craziness, there would be so much less suffering and destruction in the world. Humans solve problems far better than any other life-form but our craziness interferes profoundly with that process at every level. It is in the family, the workplace, and the politics of humankind that we see the colossal waste and pain of our proclivity for destructive dysfunctionality.[39]

That "craziness" has a root cause: free riding. It inflicts mortal psycho-social and environmental wounds, no matter what kind of political jurisdiction may prevail (democratic or authoritarian), or the mode of economic organisation (capitalist or communist). Rent seeking has mutated into its cannibalistic phase. It is now devouring what energy remains in those who are still trying to add value by their labour.

---

38. https://blogs.imf.org/2019/04/04/tackling-corruption-in-government
39. Stephen M. Johnson (1994), *Character Styles*, New York: Norton, p.xvi.

CHAPTER EIGHT

The Culture of Cannibalism

Collapse is embedded in the DNA of a civilisation that normalises free riding. The de-socialisation of Rent, and the taxation of wages, exacts a high price: degradation of the Social Galaxy. Humanity is shredded as the mortal effects cascade through personalities and communities. The legacy assets that people needed to postpone nature's law of entropy are systematically exhausted.

In nature, the 2nd Law of Thermodynamics traces the gravitational pull of energy towards the state of entropy. Energy is degraded and transformed into a state of disorder. In the Social Galaxy, this effect is offset by what I called the 1st Law of Social Dynamics.

> So long as people kept the umbilical 1st Law in good working order, they would be safe. There would be food, clothing and shelter for those willing to work with nature to continue procreating. They learnt how to handle the challenges that came with consciousness. They employed first-person empirical methods to hone the social and moral rules that would guide them as they migrated through time and space. The outcomes were durable, and applied to everyone who contributed to the gene pool.[6]

---

6. Fred Harrison (2012), *The Traumatised Society*, London: Shepheard-Walwyn, p.19.

The evolutionary push of the 1st Law is in the direction of growth through creativity. That growth is thrown into reverse when free riding is allowed to triumph over the people who work to fulfil their personal and social needs. Western civilisation has now arrived at that state.

A society that begins to devour itself is locked into a state of cannibalism. Cannibalism is the Social Galaxy's equivalent to nature's 2nd Law. The thermal properties of the population are dissipated to the point where it becomes impossible to support free riding behaviour. Free riders, confronted with that crisis, become desperate. Instead of reducing their demands, their insatiable appetites over-ride the survival instinct. They proceed to devour the subsistence that is required to sustain the working population at a minimum biological level of existence. Stasis sets in. This renders communities vulnerable to external predators. This is a dangerous situation, with free riders now incapable of defending the borders of the territories on which they rely for their free meals. Defeat is inevitable. History is replete with such episodes.

Philosophers of the Scottish Enlightenment could not have predicted the date on which the West would reach the precipice. By the mid-19th century, however, it was possible to hear the alarm bells ringing. Drawing on Adam Smith, the contours of the culture of cheating could have been identified. Rebasing governance on the nation's net income would have diverted the West away from the tipping point. The evidence was abundant, and the tools were available to decode what was happening. Instead, the vital signs were ignored in the centres of learning.

Typical was the tragedy stemming from the decision to build Marischal College in Aberdeen. The monumental structure in Broad Street became one of Britain's pre-eminent centres of scholarship. One of its professors was the creator of Maxwell's Demon, whom we met in the Prologue. Historian Michael Dey records the human price that was paid for the construction of that centre of learning. People were evicted from their homes to make way for the granite slabs. "No provision was made to house them, however – a failure to act described by the local press as 'a most inhuman proceeding'. Thrown on the streets with few resources," the evicted families could not afford the rents of the alternative dwellings.[7] By then, the culture of cheating had inoculated the law-makers against the pain of the dispossessed. So the boom/bust process in the property market was free to continue wrecking its way into the 20th century until, today, the tipping point has arrived.

The Experts remained silent. Those who study existential risks confine their investigations to technology, climate change, asteroids from outer space and biogenetics.[8] Mundane transactions in the property market do not feature in their algorithms. Analytical frameworks ignore the cultural field that incubates the cannibalism to which free riding eventually gravitates. Scientists who study society fail to profile that culture for what it is.

▶ *Irresponsible:* refusing to be held accountable for wrecking people's lives.

▶ *Insatiable:* an all-devouring lust for the living tissue of humanity.

▶ *Insensitive:* immune to the pain inflicted on victims.

The human sensibilities that served as defensive mechanisms had been blunted.

▶ *Desensitised:* the dispossessed were schooled into serving as lapdogs of the upper class (recall the armies of servants in the "big houses").

7. Michael Dey (2018), *The Granite City*, Stroud: Amberley, p.49.
8. Nick Bostrom and Milan M. Cirkovic (2008), Eds., *Global Catastrophic Risks*, Oxford: Oxford University Press.

► *Deracinated:* the traditions that secured people's rights were uprooted, weakening the resilience needed to negotiate treacherous times.

► *Detached:* the land-grabbers anaesthetised their consciences by dropping crumbs from the top table to smother moral and mental capacities.

The process of erosion continues to this day, the beneficiaries of rent seeking carefully crafting the social narrative to protect their vital interests. In Britain, the elites remain alert, distracting awareness of class distinctions in the era of universal suffrage. A study of more than 70,000 entrants in *Who's Who* revealed how, since 1897, the upper class had shifted their declared interests from traditional aristocratic or highbrow pursuits (hunting, opera) to ordinary interests (pets, pop music).[9] The intention was to "indicate their 'ordinariness' as they become increasingly sensitive to public opinion in an era of rising inequality".[10] The subliminal purpose: convince people that free riders were no different from "ordinary" folk!

Laws and institutions are crafted to create Kafkaesque situations that leave people bewildered. Oppressive institutions conflict with people's perceptions of "the facts" on the ground. Franz Kafka (1883–1924) explored such psychodramas in his novels. Culpability is concealed with the aid of the kinetic power of words. An example is the way in which international financial institutions are interpreting the bleak prospects for the millennial generation (Box 8.1).

---

9. Peter Scott and James T. Walker (2020), "The Comfortable, the Rich, and the Super-Rich. What Really Happened to Top British Incomes during the First Half of the Twentieth Century?" *J of Econ History*, 80(1).
10. http://www.lse.ac.uk/News/Latest-news-from-LSE/2020/d-April-20/Elites-swap-highbrow-culture-for-ordinary-pursuits-in-their-public-profiles

---

Box 8.1 **Shifting responsibility**

Employment prospects for young people have swung into reverse. Agencies that are supposed to diagnose and prescribe remedies are resigned to current realities.

In a study of life chances in the West, IMF economists claim that the decline in material welfare is attributable to technology and globalisation. The young are victims, despite attaining a higher level of education than their parents.*

People born between 1980 and 2000 face an insecure working life and diminished prospects when they reach retirement age. The best advice offered by the IMF: get even more education and hope to avoid the "hollowing out" of the middle classes. Blame for the bleak prospects is attributed to trends that ought to be celebrated as progressive – labour-saving technology, and deeper economic partnerships with people in other parts of the world.

Missing from the diagnosis is a vision of how those trends could (under amended circumstances) enhance, rather than diminish, life chances. Instead, young people are invited to resign themselves to not even matching – let alone improving on – the quality of their parents' lives.

* Era Dabla-Norris (2020), The Declining Fortunes of the Young, Feb. 27. https://blogs.imf.org/2020/02/27/the-declining-fortunes-of-the-young/?utm_medium=email&utm_source=govdelivery

---

In our post-truth world, it is dangerous to believe what you see or hear. But it is equally dangerous to challenge the versions authorised by those who sustain the deceptions. This is an impossible situation. Should we heed the warnings offered by the fossils in museum archives?

The Dynamics of F>R

In one important respect, humans are not unique. Over the past hundred million years, a succession of species evolved to dominate their environments. They were wiped out by shifts in geological structures, oceanic flows and atmospheric temperatures. From the dinosaurs to the great apes and all the way to the Neanderthals who roamed Europe until the arrival of modern humans, the bones of extinct species that were once supreme are now fossils waiting to be excavated by zoologists. The laws of physics are unremitting in seeking to inflict this fate on *Homo sapiens*.

There is a terrible irony in this state of affairs. The existential threat that we now face is not from nature. We are responsible for guiding our destiny.

The mother of all crises begins with the disorder denoted by the equation F>R.

Prime characteristics of free riding include irresponsible behaviour, insatiable acquisitiveness and the self-centred disregard for others. When the rate and depth of penetration of free riding (denoted by the letter F) reaches the point where it eclipses the rate at which people are capable of producing net income (R, for Rent), society falls victim to cannibalism. F>R. This cannibalism is self-destroying: free riding devours the means of its own existence.

If humanity is to survive at this 11th hour, institutionalised cheating needs to be extinguished. F>R must be reversed into F<R, to herald the beginning of the end of free riding. But is the present crisis really terminal? That is the conclusion from three realms of our existence.

F>R (1)

Anthropocene is the name of the geological age which acknowledges human impact on Earth. Nature is now reclaiming its domain.

Nature could tolerate the intrusion of an alien galaxy for so long as humans treated the universe with respect. But the rate at which we are extinguishing other species denotes disrespect for life on Earth. Plastic coating of the oceans makes life intolerable for aquatic species. Such irresponsible behaviour triggers geophysical ruptures to the planet on a scale that is provoking violent reactions. The melting of arctic ice will flood hundreds of coastal cities. Such events, in turn, affect mortality rates: outdoor air pollution caused 4.2m premature deaths worldwide in 2016, according to the World Health Organisation (WHO).[6]

F>R (2)

Governance is impotent when it is not trusted by the majority of people. The Great Rejection is called populism.

People are turning away from mainstream politics in favour of anything that offers emotional relief from the sense of frustration and deprivation. In the US, populism enabled the disruptive rent-seeker Donald Trump to enter the White House in 2017. He exploited the dissatisfaction driven by, for example, the decline in average life expectancy. America's mortality crisis is infecting the rest of the world.[7] Averages conceal the far worse prospects for people confined in towns along the rust belt.[8] From the US, the opioid crisis is spreading throughout the world. The Centre for the Future of Democracy, at the University of Cambridge, tracks views on democracy based on 4m people in 3,500 surveys. In 2019, the proportion dissatisfied with democracy rose from 48% to 58%. The UK and the US led the decline in trust with the highest levels of discontent.[9]

6. https://www.who.int/news-room/fact-sheets/detail/ambient-(outdoor)-air-quality-and-health
7. Anne Case and Angus Deaton (2020), "The Epidemic of Despair", *Foreign Affairs*, March/April.
8. Michael Lind (2020), *The New Class War*, London: Penguin.
9. https://www.bbc.co.uk/news/education-51281722

Social psychologists do not analyse the rack-renting of the collective consciousness. Instead, mental ill-health or violent behaviour are treated as the quirks of individuals, to be viewed either with sympathy or the strong arm of the law, or ignored because the resources are not available to contain the damage that is inflicted on souls and society.

F > R (3)

Globalism is converted into a scapegoat. This inspires nationalism, the ideology that accommodates rent seeking.

Globalisation could improve the lives of everyone, but is bedevilled by animosities aimed at "the other". One political response is to threaten military action, which distracts home-based discontent. One cause of mass civil disobedience is the inability of poorer countries to catch up with high-income nations. The World Bank notes the slowdown in growth in low-income countries as the "steepest, longest and broadest yet".[10] Globalisation has lost its attractions as a way to cut costs of production and raise net income, but the international financial agencies fail to explain that the problem is not with international trade. The core issue is with the failure to share the net incomes with every person, and every nation, that created the global Rents. How could it have been otherwise? The driving force in Europe's history since 1500 was the predatory behaviour that enriched the West by plundering other people's rent-yielding natural assets.

Gouging people's cultures

Slavery was a leading driver of enrichment for European elites in countries like France and the Netherlands. The trade in goods generated by slaves, which fuelled trade across the globe from

---

10.. World Bank (2020), *Global Economic Prospects: Slow Growth, Policy Challenges*, Washington, DC.

the East Indies to South America, was equivalent to about 11% of the British economy by the early 19th century.[11] But statistical computations by researchers do not capture the formative influence of slavery on the character of the European economy. The processes and attitudes that drive economic relations in the 21st century were shaped by state-sponsored pirates. Leading the way were the scavengers who sailed the high seas on a mission that laid the foundations of the most expansive empire in history. J.M. Keynes provided the broad-brush strokes to illuminate that process.

Recall the historical context. First, monarchs and their nobilities grabbed and privatised the land. This impoverished the working population and created the binary culture that became the capitalist mode of production (Box 8.2). Then, the state was adapted with funds accumulated by robbing the Rent that other nations – notably Spain – had stolen from indigenous peoples in South America. And so, the United Kingdom was fashioned to fund the territorial expansion into what became a global empire.

Keynes followed the financial trail in *A Treatise on Money*. He pointed out that "the booty brought back by Drake in the *Golden Hind* may fairly be considered the foundation and origin of British Foreign Investment". Elizabeth I paid off her foreign debt and invested a part of the balance – about £42,000 – in the Levant Company. The profits from the Levant Company funded the creation of the East India Company, the profits from which, in turn, during the 17th and 18th centuries, "were the main foundation of England's foreign connections; and so on".[12]

Keynes analysed the economics of state-sponsored piracy. First, there was the acceleration of productive activity, and the

---

11. Klas Rönnbäck (2018), "On the economic importance of the slave plantation complex to the British economy during the 18th century: a value-added approach", *J. of Global History*, 13. https://doi.org/10.1017/S1740022818000177

12. J.M. Keynes (1953), *A Treatise on Money*, Vol. 2, London: Macmillan, pp.156-158.

Box 8.2 **Demonising the dispossessed**

An Australian soldier/lawyer offered a forensic account of this transition from value-adding to rent seeking, and he accurately defined it as capitalism. Major General Sir William John Victor Windeyer, KBE, CB, DSO & Bar (1900–1987) was a barrister who became a judge of the High Court of Australia. In lectures at the University of Sydney, he did not mince his words when he described the emergence of the modern politico-economic system in England.

> The spoliation of the monastery lands increased the tendency of the land-holding class to become capitalists with tenant farmers who worked their land with hired labourers. The profits of sheep grazing continued to turn arable land to pasture and to render ploughmen unemployed.

Capitalism was incubated in the period that saw the theft of traditional rights of access to land held in common in the villages of England. The vicious free riding virus was unleashed. Windeyer notes the consequences.

> Paupers and sturdy beggars whom the law called "rogues and vagabonds" came upon the stage. The Poor Law and the Vagrancy Acts began.*

Henry VIII used the law to demonise landless peasants as vagrants (22 Hen. VIII, c.12). His ruthless state initiated repressive penal statutes against failed debtors, the first of which was enacted in 1543, followed by a Vagrancy Act (1547). Dispossessed of the commons and left to beg and steal their way along the highways, the law bore down on them without sympathy.

Windeyer explained to his students that vagrants were classified as "idle and disorderly persons" and "rogues and vagabonds". Under the law of England, those who were arrested were turned into slaves for two years, beaten and chained, bought and sold, and fed a diet of bread and water. Their counterparts, today, are begging and sleeping in the streets of towns across the UK.

The earlier vagrancy Acts were consolidated in 1824 (5 Geo. IV, c.83).

* W.J.V. Windeyer (1938), *Lectures on Legal History*, Sydney: The Law Book Company, p.141.

diversification away from agriculture. What mattered was not the value of the booty – perhaps, in total, not more than £3m – but the way in which it helped to fund "the increment of the country's wealth in buildings and improvements". The net income produced by indigenous peoples on other continents fructified within the shores of the British Isles. Keynes did not deconstruct the statistics to trace how the net income from such investments mutated into privately appropriated Rent within the British Isles. But he did not ignore the human costs which, to this day, are omitted from national balance sheets. Rack-renting the peoples of England, Ireland, Scotland and Wales (the process of depleting the human condition which we analysed in Ch.4), supplemented the Rent racked out of the people who laboured in foreign pastures.

> [T]he hardship to the agricultural population...became a serious problem in the later years of Elizabeth [I], due to prices outstripping wages; for it was out of this reduced standard of life, as well as out of increased economic activity (tempered by periodic years of crisis and unemployment), that the accumulation of capital was partly derived.

Thanks to the "magic" of compound interest, Britain became an empire. As Keynes noted, "the £42,000 invested by Elizabeth of Drake's booty in 1580 would have accumulated by 1930 to approximately the actual aggregate of our present foreign investments, namely £4,200,000,000 – or, say, 100,000 times greater than the original investment".

Humane deeds were carefully crafted to protect the culture of cheating. An example is the Slavery Abolition Act (1833). Slave owners were paid £20m in compensation, or £23bn in 2020 values, reports Deryck Browne, author of *Black people, mental health & the courts* (1990). That compensation became a "fiscal stimulus [that] built railways, hospitals, political dynasties and banking dynasties, embedding the brutal legacy of slavery into the very fabric of British society".[13]

---

13. Deryck Browne (2020), Letter, *Daily Telegraph*, June 11.

This process was *not* a "free market" at work. It was predatory economics based on the Propensity to Plunder. Transforming European nations into their "developed" status was not the product of intelligence. Intelligence is a capacity nurtured over evolutionary timescales by the purposeful investment of net income.

The enrichment of Europe was the outcome of a savage combination of political, military and diplomatic strategies grounded in the abuse of power. Since 1500, the Rent generated in colonised territories was imported into Europe and invested, in part, in the skills needed to keep abreast of new Rent-yielding technologies. Materially, the West flourished, but the plundered nations were impoverished.

Not everyone in the West grew rich. Many of the peasants who lost their livelihoods to the nobility were left desperate. The homeless vagabonds were harassed by Parliament (as with its 1597 Vagabond Act).

Some of the rootless men heard about the treasures being captured by the state-sponsored pirates, so they embarked on careers as privateers on the high seas. They faced two problems. One was the wrath of the British state: privateers were stealing loot that would otherwise have gone into the government's coffers, so they were hounded across the seven seas. The other proble was intimately framed by nature's 2nd Law. Not only were they hungry and in need of the sustenance that could be stolen from vessels sailing under the flags of other nations or the British East India Company. There was a time limit on the seaworthiness of their sailing boats. Without refits, the wooden hulls could be destroyed in four or five months by shipworms. But because they were outlaws, the privateers could not use dry docks.

Careening was the only option: deliberately ground a ship on a beach at high tide, exposing one side of the hull so that the damage inflicted by shipworms – and by other quiet nemeses like barnacles and rot – could be undone.[14]

And so, by means fair or foul, the leading European nation-states were born by rack-renting not only the indigenous peoples on other continents; but by plundering the culture of their own peoples, a process which continues to this day.

Gouging people's minds

One legacy of the culture of cheating is the reduction in the average level of intelligence. IQ increased up to the late 1970s because the Welfare State was able to devote resources to education and nutrition to enhance people's lives. Then, the process of plunder reasserted itself, and the gains enjoyed under the protection of the Welfare State went into reverse.

In assessing the decline in IQ in some European nations over the period 1950-2000, Richard Lynn concluded that this trend "will spread to economically developing countries and the whole world will move into a period of declining genotypic and phenotypic intelligence".[15] Other scientists support the view that this trend will continue throughout the 21st century (the decline in IQ is stylistically depicted in Figure 8.1). The condition of humanity will continue to deteriorate while its living tissue – Rent – is degraded.

In the UK, the mental health of the population is plummeting. An associated symptom is a reversal of the trend in life expectancy. Sir Michael Marmot, who heads the Institute of Health Equity at University College London, assembled the evidence. In his

14. Steven Johnson (2020), *Enemy of all Mankind: A True Story of Piracy, Power and History's First Global Manhunt*, New York: Riverhead Books, p.118.
15. Richard Lynn and John Harvey (2008), "The decline of the world's IQ", *Intelligence* 36, pp.112–120. DOI: 10.1016/j.intell.2007.03.004

Figure 8.1 **World IQ 1950-2040**

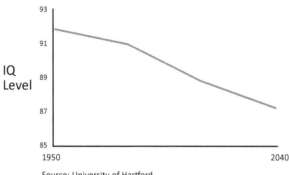

Source: University of Hartford

assessment of the health of the nation, he highlighted rising child poverty, the decline in spending on education, an increase in zero-hours employment contracts and the large numbers of people who, to survive, have to resort to food banks for their subsistence. The cumulative effect is the reversal of life expectancy, which is more pronounced in low-income regions of the country.[16]

> I'm not saying 'austerity is killing people'. I'm saying it's highly likely –
> because we identified the key drivers of health and health inequalities,
> and because they've changed in an adverse direction – that those
> changes are responsible for the health effects that we see.[17]

Marmot estimated the deadweight costs of the policies that created these situations: about £80bn every year in lost revenue and the increased cost of hospitals and welfare.

The popular belief is that these outcomes are result of austerity policies imposed after the 2008 financial crisis. In reality, austerity

---

16. *Health Equity in England: The Marmot Review 10 years on*, London: Institute of Health Equity, p.13. https://www.health.org.uk/publications/reports/the-marmot-review-10-years-on
17. Sarah Neville (2020), "Life expectancy increased stalled after decade of austerity", *Financial Times*, Feb. 25.

was the proximate, not the root, cause. If we wish to isolate the virus that is causing these tragic outcomes, we have to turn to the financial system that is servile to free riding.

The Sutton Trust, a UK educational charity, highlighted one example of the Rent effect. It examined the impact of location on education. The best-performing schools were located in areas where families could afford to pay a premium to live in the roads that gave their children access to high-quality education. One outcome: an average 6.9% gap in the academic quality between schools attended by poor and non-poor pupils. This was "a very substantial effect".[18] High house prices confirm that the net gains from good education are captured as location Rents.

The decline in IQ can be reversed by increasing the resources devoted to education and the nutrition of children.[19] That, however, only becomes possible with a paradigm shift away from the finances that favour the culture of cheating.

The spacetime conundrum

We ought to be able to track the degradation of culture, and the health of people's minds, with the aid of data on Rent. Government statisticians do not compute Rent – as defined by the classical economists – so diagnosis has to rely on proxies.

We gain a sense of the trends from the classification of people based on their incomes. Figure 8.2 tracks the savings glut in the USA. The break with the past occurred in the 1970s. Savings accumulated by the Top 1% rose to astronomical heights. The Bottom 90% fell deeper into debt. Figure 8.3 displays the division in terms of debtors and creditors. The vast majority of

---

18. Simon Burgess et al (2020), *School Places: A Fair Choice?* London: The Sutton Trust, p.7.
19. Bernt Bratsberga and Ole Rogeberga (2018), "Flynn effect and its reversal are both environmentally caused", PNAS, 115(26), pp. 6674–6678.

Figure 8:2 **The US savings glut**

Savings of groups in the US income distribution
as a % of national income

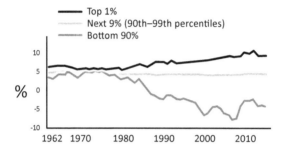

Figure 8.3 **US Creditors and debtors**

Changes in net household debt as a share of national income
relative to 1982, across the US income distribution (% points)

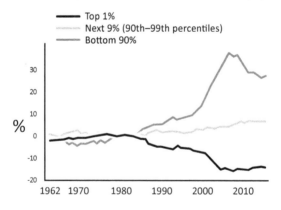

Source: Atif Mian, Ludwig Straub and Amir Sufi (2020), The Saving Glut of the Rich and the Rise in Household Debt", NBER Working Paper No. 26941. Based on Figures 6 and 15. https://www.nber.org/papers/w26941

people have to borrow from the 1% in order to live: the majority are financial hostages to a handful of fellow citizens.

The flow of energy on which the Social Galaxy depends for its existence has been exhausted. The victory of the culture of cheating, however, is pyrrhic. The ultimate victim is free riding itself. By annexing space as its private property, it detached three components of the rent seeking society from the realities of time.

▶ *The free riders:* Rent-seekers sought immortality by treating time as eternity. Family dynasties were forever, traced in oil paintings draped on the walls of palatial homes. Space was taken for granted, so long as the Rents came rolling in. They lost sight of their precarious condition as parasites on the body politic, oblivious of the erosion of the ability of worker bees to produce the honey on which they feasted.

▶ *The dispossessed:* Locked into survival mode, time became meaningless in the scramble to maintain biological existence. Space was the precarious edge of habitations that they could not afford. Relegated to anonymous status, their existence was monitored in the Births, Deaths and Marriages records – so that the rent seeking state could enforce its tax-taking powers.

▶ *The Social Galaxy:* Disorientated, the system lost is evolutionary, creative momentum. Time was thrown into reverse. The pillars on which humanity was constructed – the material, moral and mental assets funded out of Rent – atrophied, as Rent was relentlessly converted into the self-aggrandising rewards of the culture of cheating.

Some of the material remnants of the original free riders are venerated in the UK as "national treasures". The National Trust conserves some of the monumental homes of the aristocracy.

The original occupants – rack-renters, slave owners and territorial conquerors – are revered as the scions of a modern nation. Portraits of their long-dead family pets, enshrined in oil on canvas, are displayed on sideboards. Absent from view are the people who laboured "beneath stairs" to maintain these palatial Rent-funded monuments in working order.[20]

The formation of free riders as a class was a necessary device. This not only gave them power over the "lower orders". It also insulated their psyches from the painful consequences of their actions. But this detachment from reality would one day prove to be the undoing of their culture. The instinct for recognising the danger to their vital interests was blunted. With unlimited appetites, they gorged on the value-adding capacities of the Social Galaxy, burrowing deeper into the foundations of humanity to the point where they were cannibalising the means of their own existence. By driving the culture of cheating into the surreal art of "making money out of thin air", they rode blindly towards the precipice. They failed to recognise the tipping point, when the rate of Rent appropriation exceeded the rate at which net income was produced: F>R.

But suddenly, out of China, came a mortal virus. Might this intervention be a stay of execution for the culture of cheating?

Revival of the spacetime equation

My portrait of western civilisation is painful. It is tempting to seek comfort in the state of denial. How dare we characterise as decadence the high cultural accomplishments of the past five

---

20. The exception proves the rule. Erdigg is an estate on the Welsh border where generations of the Yorke family drew much of their Rent from coal. Respect was displayed for the servants. Beginning in 1793, and proceeding well into the 20th century, oil paintings of servants, kitchen porters, carpenters, gamekeepers and retired housekeepers were commissioned and hung on the walls of the "big house". https://www.nationaltrust.org.uk/erddig/features/18th-century-erddig-incentive-scheme-or-homespun-legacy

centuries? We can see the artistic creations, hear the symphonies, relish the literature, and even soar away with the science that has made travel to the moon possible.

Jacques Barzun, the French-American historian, catalogued that cultural record in his monumental *From Dawn to Decadence*. In fine detail, he pieces together the fabulous achievements of what he calls "the mongrel civilization" of the West. Analysing the trends that began in 1500, he concludes that decadence arrived at the end of the 20th century with the loss of what he calls Possibility.

> The forms of art as of life seem exhausted, the stages of development have been run through. Institutions function painfully. Repetition and frustration are the intolerable result. Boredom and fatigue are great historical forces.[21]

We cannot audit the value of the achievements against the wholesale destruction of other people's cultures, the raping of their habitats, the deaths by diseases and wars inflicted on defenceless indigenous populations, to arrive at "the bottom line". How do we assess the value of what the people of Europe lost – a value that they would have produced if the free riding virus had been stillborn in the 16th century? What might have been created is the stuff of dreams. If only; if only the evolution of the Social Galaxy had continued along a peaceful trajectory, as people deepened the potential in their minds, bodies and souls.

But wait. Even at this late hour, might the pandemic of 2020 be the spark that ignites an effective demand for an end to "business-as-usual"?

---

21. Jacques Barzun (2000), *From Dawn to Decadence*, London: HarperCollins, p.xvi.

WE ARE RENT

The Indictments

Armed with the facts, the three indictments that I presented in the introduction may now be interrogated.

My overarching thesis asserts that the conversion of social Rent into private income results in the systematic sacrifice of the right of everyone to work for, and enjoy, equal access to the Good Life, and to the further evolution of their communities. Did I substantiate this proposition to the point where reform is now imperative?

The urgent need for change arises from the fact that European societies are disorientated. This state of affairs is the result of the cumulative impacts of the property rights favoured by their feudal aristocracies. They chose to live as free riders. Today, everyone is vulnerable to the existential crises that are converging (the timing and trends are documented in the Prologue to Book 2).

The systemic fractures were exposed to public gaze by Covid-19. We take the pandemic of 2020 as a starting point for this inquest. I will continue to illustrate the problems common to all societies with facts as they relate to the UK.

The Johnson administration closed the economy to save lives. People initially accepted that material security had to be sacrificed to minimise the number of deaths. Emergency hospitals were created because, it was feared, the National Health Service (NHS) would be overwhelmed with patients infected by the virus. That response was driven by humane considerations: beds should be reserved for Covid-19 patients. The political strategy, however, was not grounded in all of the relevant facts. As a consequence, many people with other life-threatening diseases died needlessly. Among the collateral victims were cancer patients and those who contracted heart and circulatory diseases.[1]

The "excess deaths" and the suffering from postponed medical treatment were not the price of a humane reaction to the pandemic. They were needless. They were the direct result of attitudes and practices that stemmed from the tenure-and-tax policies which had pulverised the productive capacity of the population. By refusing to employ optimum policies for raising revenue, politicians through the generations had to adopt debt as an instrument of governance. Then, to "balance the books", savage cuts in funding had to be inflicted on social services.

By choosing taxes that distort people's behaviour, and distort the distribution of national income, government revenue falls short of national need. One result: retrenchment on the resources allocated to protect health. Before the arrival of the virus from China, the cash cut-backs also reduced the quality of service provided by the UK's schools, the law enforcement agencies and the capacities of the civil service.

A comprehensive audit would add up the deadweight losses attributable to the perverse tax regime. The bottom line would provoke public outrage. That is why such an audit does not feature in the calculations offered by HM Treasury when it lodges its annual budget in Parliament. So:

---

1. The "excess deaths" were monitored by, among others, the British Heart Foundation. https://www.bhf.org.uk/what-we-do/news-from-the-bhf/news-archive/2020/october/rise-in-excess-heart-and-circulatory-disease-deaths-in-under-65s

1. *Many deaths, and economic losses, were intentional because they were avoidable*

2. *Many people born since 2000 will suffer needlessly for the rest of their lives*

3. *Politicians escape accountability by sustaining the culture of deception*

In the court of public opinion, who could be trusted to bear witness to these charges? As a contribution to the formation of that opinion, I will offer the views of three witnesses.

The unsilenced voices

I have dedicated this book to the memory of three colleagues who devoted themselves to championing the reforms that would equalise people's life-chances. Based on their writings and my conversations with them, it is my privilege to make their presence felt. I will review the consequences of the culture of cheating under three headings.

Deaths on the altar of free riding

Witness: Dr. George Miller
Epidemiologist, Medical Research Council's
Senior Clinical Scientific Staff

Dr Miller's book *On Fairness and Efficiency* was assessed as "the life work of a genius of the social sciences".[2] Miller's credentials as an epidemiologist were of the highest order. Politicians will be disturbed by his verdict on whether they can be trusted with the welfare of the people.

---

2. Mason Gaffney (2011), review of George Miller (2000), *On Fairness and Efficiency*, Bristol: Policy Press, in *Groundswell*, March-April, p.8. http://www.cooperative-individualism.org/gaffney-mason_review-of-george-miller-on-fairness-and-efficiency-2011-mar-apr.pdf

Law-makers are endowed with power to protect their constituents. How, wondered Dr Miller, could this be squared with the fact that, in England and Wales alone, the public's revenue system was responsible for killing about 50,000 people every year? Epidemiologists class these as "excess deaths". The explanation for the deaths offered by Miller, however, is not discussed by his colleagues.

Miller's thousand-year study of the evolution of English history led him to the conclusion that the many proximate causes of premature death (think tobacco's link to cancer) were just the ripples that originated with the tax tools favoured by governments.

> Perhaps as many as 50,000 people die prematurely every year in England and Wales because of the effects of Britain's discriminatory socio-economic system, which hurts the poor more than the rich. These unnecessary deaths can ultimately be traced back to the method government uses to raise revenue. The causal chain linking health, wealth and taxation policy may be complicated, but in my judgement it is definitely established.[3]

These fatalities are characterised as "deaths by despair" by Angus Deaton (see Ch.5, p.99). But why were so many people living in despair? It is not sufficient to observe that they lived in poverty, which is not a voluntary condition. Why were generations of people – all of them willing to work for their living - consigned to a state of permanent subsistence?

The UK has the lowest healthy life expectancy in Western Europe, according to the Global Burden of Disease study.[4] In an editorial, *The Lancet* asked: "Have health leaders and advocates been missing the most important determinants of human health?" It warned that poverty and inequality were "structural inequities" which had to be "tackled".[5] But it offered no clues as to the nature

3. George J. Miller (2003), *Dying for Justice,* London: Centre for Land Policy Studies, p.1.
4. *The Lancet* (2020), *Global Burden of Disease Study 2019* (396).
5. Editorial (2020), "Global health: time for radical change?" *The Lancet,* 396, October 17. www.thelancet.com

of the structure that was inequitably skewed against people on low or no incomes. In the academic literature, the concept of the structure is readily used without defining it in terms of the pillars on which society is constructed.

What does "structure" denote? One feature is the framework of authority that empowers people to achieve their needs and aspirations. The authority structure shapes the institutions that mediate relationships between people and the techniques for enforcing the rules. If the authority system facilitates the pooling of resources that can be devoted to funding services for the common good, the nature of the public's pricing mechanism supports people's behaviour. The ripples are transmitted inter-generationally. This is the structure that epidemiologists – apart from George Miller – are loath to probe.

In a society structured on inequitable foundations, poverty is not the cause of deadly diseases: it is one of the ripples from the rules that rupture relationships and distort behaviour. Those ripples emerge as stresses in the employment market; in the cost of shelter and in the distribution of savings. These are involuntary stresses that do *not* (ordinarily) stem from personal failures. Today, however, the welter of statistics on poverty and inequality beguile the analysts who settle for the easy diagnoses. That accommodates the desire of politicians for quick remedies. The statistics, however, leave many questions unanswered.

Why, for example, was the Covid infection rate higher in the north of England than in the south? Scholars noted the higher rates of poverty, housing densities and unemployment levels that rendered northerners more vulnerable to the virus. But since these communities did not voluntarily adopt the socio-economic and spatial conditions that rendered them vulnerable – why were they forced to endure this state of affairs?

In his analysis, George Miller did not confine himself to using the conventional modelling tools employed by epidemiologists to explain disease and death. His forensic study of England left him in no doubt that responsibility for the premature deaths lay with governments. Those deaths were logical outcomes of policies favoured by politicians on both the left and the right of the ideological spectrum. Thus, before Covid-19 struck, healthy life expectancy at birth rose to 68.9 years (2018). The expectation in Wandsworth, London, rose by an extra six years. For babies born in Stockton-on-Tees and Darlington, in the north-east corner of England, the prognosis was the reverse: a significant 6% fall in the average life expectancy.

How do we explain this spatial contrast? Epidemiologist John Newton, a member of the Global Burden of Disease Scientific Council, drew on place-based discrepancies to observe that "people in the richest areas enjoy 19 more years in good health than those in the poorest".

> As well as being unfair, health inequalities are costly, putting a strain on employment and productivity, hitting national and local economies and impacting our public services...the extra cost of inequalities to the NHS have been calculated as £4.8 billion a year in greater hospitalisations alone.[6]

People who live in some of the deprived neighbourhoods lose as much as 12 years of life.

If the social structure is designed to operate inclusively, in the best interests of the population, the outcomes are optimal. If anti-social forces are allowed to tamper with the structure, the ripple effects are transmitted from the centre of power to the farthest edges of the community.

In *Ricardo's Law*, I traced the trends in the form of a journey across the UK. The drive northwards from London along the ancient Roman Road traverses seven statistical regions.

6. John Newton, *et al* (2019), "Enabling joint action to reduce health inequalities". https://publichealthmatters.blog.gov.uk/2019/07/29/enabling-joint-action-to-reduce-health-inequalities/

Table E.1. **UK life expectancy: years (2016 to 2018)***

	Males	Females	Average House Price: £†
London	80.7	84.5	489,159
South-East	80.7	84.1	332,147
East of England	80.3	83.7	296,411
East Midlands	79.4	82.9	202,345
Yorkshire & Humber	78.7	82.4	170,025
North-east	77.9	81.7	131,701
Scotland	77.1	81.1	155,191

* ONS (2019), Health state life expectancies, UK: 2016 to 2018, Table 1, p.3.
† August 2020, from Office for National Statistics: www.ons.gov.uk/

The longest lives combine with the highest land values in London. From the capital, it is a downhill decline in life expectancy, along with the decline in land values. The data in Table E.1 show the decline persisting across the border into Scotland. House prices serve as proxies for land values. The cost of building a home is similar across the country: the difference is in the Rental value assigned to land.

Epidemiologists characterise such data as correlations. In fact, it reveals the starting point for a chain of causation at work that penetrates every part of our lives. But can we fairly claim that the outcomes are *intentional?*

Dereliction of Government Duty

Witness: Mason Gaffney
Professor of Economics, University of California

We first met Dr Gaffney in Chapter 5 (p.86). His work focused on a whole-of-life approach to governance. Only by monitoring all of the impacts of public servants – and private citizens – can we achieve a robust assessment of society. Rent was the metric for that monitoring exercise. Gaffney worked into his 90s to implore policy-makers to recognise that their deadweight taxes rendered them guilty of a dereliction of duty towards their constituents. Their taxes were not retained for rational reasons: they penalised the working population while rewarding free riding behaviour.

The terms of the whole-of-life model of economics favoured by Gaffney were an open secret. He stressed that the socio-economic and ecological problems persist solely because those entrusted with political power fail to learn the lessons of history. That law-makers chose to ignore those lessons, even when the lessons were as recent as 2008, is illustrated by the behaviour of Boris Johnson, the Prime Minister who presided over the pandemic in Britain.

Some of the key facts were highlighted by Mariana Mazzucato, an American Professor of Economics at University College London. In a post-mortem article on "Capitalism after the Pandemic", she highlighted the economy's "structural flaws".[7] In the West, real estate lending rose from about 35% of all bank lending in 1970 to 60% by 2007. This was driven by the pursuit of capital gains from the land beneath people's residences. One outcome was the sub-prime mortgage scandal which triggered the boom that led to the bust in 2008.

The intentional nature of the "deaths by despair" is illustrated by Johnson's promise to "level up" the deprived northern regions. One strategy was intended to "fix" the problem of unaffordable mortgages. "A huge number of people feel totally excluded from capitalism, from the idea of home ownership, which is so vital for our society. And we're going to fix that – the Generation Buy is what we're going for."[8] His government resolved to encourage 5% fixed-

7. https://www.foreignaffairs.com/articles/united-states/2020-10-02/capitalism-after-covid-19-pandemic
8. Gordon Reyner (2020), "Johnson pledges to create 'Generation Buy' to get millions on property ladder", *Daily Telegraph*, October 3.

rate mortgages for low-income buyers, combined with changes to planning laws to facilitate the construction of new dwellings. But this intervention was based on the kinds of strategies that encouraged the sub-prime mortgage scandal that cost millions of people their homes when the boom/bust real estate cycle ended in 2008. That governments continue to employ such policies tells us that the law-makers have resigned themselves to intentionally endangering people's life chances.

Denial of Justice

Witness: Sir Kenneth Jupp, MC
Judge of the English High Court

According to the narrative authorised by the culture of cheating, we enjoy a world based on the "rule of law". This enshrines human rights in conventions such as the one championed by the United Nations. This narrative, however, is calibrated to deceive. When we dig deep, and assess the enforcement of those rights, we soon discover that the prosaic strictures are calculated to preserve the transfer of people's Rent to rent-seekers.

Policies hatched by participants in the Economics of the Absurd are legitimised by fantasy theories which are fabricated in academia. Professors are awarded Nobel Prizes for theoretical models that are explicitly detached from reality.[9] Has the time come for the professors to go back to their drawing boards? This is not a philosophical question, but one that entails life-and-death outcomes.

---

9. One of these is known as the M & M theorem. It was devised by two professors to encourage corporations to rely more on debt. The theorem was constructed on the assumption that the marketplace was free of frictions caused by taxation. This contribution to corporate finance did help to earn the professors their Nobel Prizes. It also contributed to the corporate debt crisis of the 21st century (because, in the real world, the impact of taxation cannot be wished away). Robin Wigglesworth (2020), "The debt bubble legacy of economists Modigliani and Miller", *Financial Times*, October 20.

Box E.1 **The Spider in the Web**

Epidemiology took centre stage across the world in 2020 as govern-ments wrestled with Covid-19. Tracing the cause of the million-plus deaths back to its roots was not contested by anyone except the Chinese Communist Party. More controversial are the causes of premature deaths that routinely afflict democratic societies.

Nancy Krieger, a Professor of Social Epidemiology at Harvard, has revealed how her profession's academics distort the research agenda.* Epidemiologists, she explains, employ models that rely on multiple causes. Those many causes were woven into a complex web. Missing from the web, however, was the "spider" – the weaver of the network of problems. This absence was achieved "by excluding any sense of history or origins, the 'web' sans 'spider' discourages epidemiologists from considering why population patterns of health and disease exist and persist or change over time".†

The web model persisted into the 21st century "chiefly to array diverse individual-level risk factors identified by biomedical and lifestyle hypotheses and does so with scant attention to the larger societal and ecologic context in which these exposures are produced and distributed".† Krieger's favoured diagnostic approach, incorporating the ecosocial framework, is the first step towards revealing the free riding virus as the spider in the body politic.

* Nancy Krieger (1994), "Epidemiology and the Web of Causation: Has anyone seen the Spider?" *Soc. Sci. Med*. 39(7), pp.892-893.
† Nancy Krieger (2011), *Epidemiology and the People's Health*, Oxford: Oxford University Press, p. 154.

The harsh realities are confronting epidemiologists who are struggling to understand the deadly lessons of Covid-19. They reject the idea that high death rates among ethnic minorities is due to genetics or racism. Rather, a report sponsored by the UK government claimed that the excess deaths were "explained by factors such as occupation, where people live, their household composition, and pre-existing health conditions". These are symptoms, not causal explanations. But the epidemiologists at least acknowledge that "a part of the excess risk 'remains unexplained'".[10] Might the virus from China finally force at least one academic discipline to come to terms with reality (see Box E.1)?

Politicians claim that they apply progressive principles to their taxes, to protect people's health and welfare. Statistics pour out of national treasuries to support the contention that governments do, indeed, formulate policies apparently directed at disadvantaged segments of their communities. Nevertheless, the combined effect of the public and private pricing systems skews the share of national income in favour of those who own rent-generating assets.

Law-makers claim that they "seek justice" for the disadvantaged members of their communities. Instead, they offer palliatives. Enter Sir Kenneth Jupp, whom we first met in Chapter 3 (p.44). Sir Kenneth explains that justice cannot be sliced and diced. There could be no half-measures. Either you enjoyed justice in its fulsome form, or you did not. Sir Kenneth, who in his work as a judge in the Queen's Bench Division respected the hard-nosed realities of legal precedents, understood that something more was needed if we were to recover a world based on justice. "Is justice to be found anywhere in this world of ours?" he asked.

Without love (by which I mean Greek *agape*, brotherly love, charity, generosity), knowledge is narrow, limited and incomplete. As love increases, knowledge also goes on increasing. Our emotions can confirm truth for us and give us direct perception of deeper truth.[11]

The deliberate narrowing of knowledge – and, therefore, the blunting of love – is a technique skilfully employed by the culture of cheating. Statistics are compiled not so much to inform, as to mislead. People are encouraged to believe that governments know what they are doing. That allows politicians who act in bad faith

10. https://www.bmj.com/content/371/bmj.m4099
11. Kenneth Jupp (2005), *The Rule of Law*, London: Shepheard-Walwyn, pp. xvi-xvii.

to escape accountability. Ordinarily, economists shy away from publishing such estimates on government performance.

A cash price can be placed on people who die needlessly. An example is the study of Covid-19 related deaths co-authored by Harvard's Larry Summers. He had served two Democratic administrations: as Treasury Secretary under President Bill Clinton, and as director of the National Economic Council under Barak Obama. He was critical of Donald Trump's handling of the virus pandemic. Writing in the *Journal of the American Medical Association*, he estimated that the pandemic imposed a loss to the US of over $16 trillion, assuming the 2020 trends continued into 2021. The cost of premature deaths of American citizens was $4.3 trillion. Long-term health impairment would cost $2.5 trillion, and mental health impairment was estimated at over $1.5 trillion.[12]

If such numbers were compiled annually, to reveal the cash cost of the tax-induced loss of life, would people mobilise to support the radical revision of their public finances in favour of a whole-of-life approach to politics? If they did so, they would transform society into one that honoured justice. Sir Kenneth insists that, under the law, justice demands "that each individual pay the nation for however much of the nation's territory he takes for his own exclusive use. To take from the universe more than one needs of anything breaches the commandment 'Thou shalt not steal'".

The vision thing

Have I offered a *prima facie* case against the power structure that underpins democratic societies? If so this becomes one starting point for the conversation about the reforms that are needed to establish trust in governance and restore resilience to communities.

---

12. David M Cutler and Lawrence H. Summers (2020), "The Covid-19 Pandemic and the $16 trillion virus". https://jamanetwork.com/journals/jama/fullarticle/2771764

The democratic consent of the people is the vaccine against the return of demagogues, who are ever ready to occupy the vacuums created by political paralysis.

National conversation is essential for the therapeutic effects of engaging in the listening-and-learning mode. Dialogue is the precursor to the redesign of the social architecture. Debates would include scrutiny of the claim that the reform of taxation must deliver the following outcomes.

1. People freed to go about their private business while honouring their social responsibilities. Pooling the Rent (with corresponding cuts in taxes on earned incomes) fulfils personal obligations to society.

2. Government revenue sufficient to fund public services. Most services are self-funding: they generate Rent which, when recycled back into the public purse, expands the resources needed to support people's aspirations.

3. Nature protected by the rent-based pricing system. By paying Rent for resources consumed, users would conserve what they did not need, while covering the costs of repairing the damage to habitats caused in the past.

How the blueprint for fiscal reform could be applied within the UK, and across the European Union, is examined in Book 2. By rebasing European civilisation on the principles of justice and evolutionary economics, a beacon would shine across the rest of the world. The global formula – One-World Rent – is explored in Book 3.

About the author

Fred Harrison is an economic forecaster and policy analyst. Ten years before the financial crisis of 2008, he alerted governments that house prices would peak in 2007, which would trigger a banking crisis and economic depression. They failed to take defensive action. Applying the same methodology, the author has assessed the impact of Covid-19 and he predicts that house prices will peak in 2026. Our world is on course for a global catastrophe, unless nations mobilise the democratic consent that is needed to adopt the financial reforms that would mitigate the looming disasters.

Harrison is a graduate of the Universities of Oxford and London. After a career in Fleet Street journalism, he turned to the study of public policy and the way in which the global community of nations had been captured by the culture that reshaped western civilisation. His *Power in the Land* (1983) set the scene for investigations leading to *The Traumatised Society* (2012). Most of his books are available on

https://shepheard-walwyn.co.uk/

To follow his campaign for a democratic reform of governance,
follow #WeAreRent
and visit www.wearerent.com

For more information on Rent, read Fred Harrison's analyses on
www.sharetherents.org

Acknowledgements

I had to travel extensively around the world to gather the materials that inform this volume. Many people kindly assisted me in that sojourn. Those who responded to requests for information for the present study include Nicolaus Tideman, Mary Cleveland, Fred Foldvary, Roger Sandilands, Dirk Löhr, Ed Dodson, Cliff Cobb, Bryan Kavanagh, Peter Meakin, Per Möller Anderson, Peter Challen and last, but not least, Heather Remoff.

I am indebted to Ian Kirkwood for his preparation of the graphics that illustrate this volume.

Valuable assistance was derived from
Land Research Trust **www.landresearchtrust.org**
The Scottish Land Revenue Group **www.slrg.scot**

Index

Windeyer, W.J.V. 158
Woodham-Smith, Cecil 71
World Bank v, 115, 138, 145, 156

X
Xi Jinping vii, 138

Y
Yeltsin, Boris 130, 132
Yi-Fu Tuan 136

Z
Zelensky, V. 146
Zuma, Jacob 145

#We Are Rent

Book 2

The Death of Democracy
And what we must do
about it

The fate of the West will be determined in 2026, predicts Fred Harrison. House prices around the world will peak, triggering the crash of the global economy. This time, unlike 2008, political and financial paralysis will drive the existential crises – environmental, demographic and military – to converge on a single catastrophic point in time. Defensive strategies can be constructed, if democratic consent can be mobilised for the reforms that would relaunch humanity back on to the evolutionary growth path. The author explains that renegotiation of the constitutions of the UK and European Union would serve as beacons of light for the rest of the world. But it is a race against time.

Forthcoming by Fred Harrison...

We Are Rent

Book 3

One-world Rent
and the Social Galaxy

The global community of nations is on course for upheavals that cannot be avoided by resurrecting the policies that have repeatedly failed in the past. One strategy alone would provide the synergy to mobilise nation-states behind the common cause of humanity. Fred Harrison explains the political significance of cross-border sharing of a stream of value which all nations help to create. One-world Rent is the blueprint that would initiate, for the first time on planet Earth, an age of inclusive peace and prosperity. Communities would be empowered to expand personal freedom while initiating new approaches to global trade and the renewal of the environment. The outcome would be a reinvigorated Social Galaxy.

Lightning Source UK Ltd.
Milton Keynes UK
UKHW020233130121
376899UK00011B/177

9 780995 635197